Cultural Heritage Conservation
in the American South

Cultural Heritage Conservation in the American South

Benita J. Howell, Editor

Southern Anthropological Society Proceedings, No. 23
Mary W. Helms, Series Editor

The University of Georgia Press
Athens and London

Southern Anthropological Society

Founded 1966

OFFICERS, 1988–89

J. Anthony Paredes, President
Andrew W. Miracle, President-Elect
Thomas A. Arcury, Secretary-Treasurer
Thomas W. Collins, Councilor
Hans A. Baer, Councilor
Patricia B. Lerch, Councilor
Mary W. Helms, Series Editor
Gifford S. Nickerson, Newsletter Editor

Program Coordinator, 1988
Thomas W. Collins

© 1990 by the Southern Anthropological Society
Published by the University of Georgia Press
Athens, Georgia 30602
All rights reserved

Set in Times Roman
The paper in this book meets the guidelines for
permanence and durability of the Committee on
Production Guidelines for Book Longevity of the
Council on Library Resources.

Printed in the United States of America

94 93 92 91 90   5 4 3 2 1

Library of Congress Cataloging in Publication Data

Cultural heritage conservation in the American South / Benita J. Howell, editor.
  p.   cm. — (Southern Anthropological Society proceedings ; no. 23)
  Papers presented at the 1988 Southern Anthropological
  Society meeting in Tampa, Florida.
  Bibliography: p.
  ISBN 0-8203-1164-2 (alk. paper).
  — ISBN 0-8203-1165-0 (pbk. : alk. paper)
  1. Cultural property, Protection of—Southern States—Congresses.
2. Southern States—Antiquities—Collection and preservation—
Congresses.   3. Indians of North America—Southern States—
Antiquities—Collection and preservation—Congresses.   4. Southern
States—Cultural policy—Congresses.   5. Southern States—
Historiography—Congresses.   I. Howell, Benita J.   II. Southern
Anthropological Society.   III. Series.
GN2.S9243 no. 23
[F211]
301 s—dc20   89-4848
[975'.01]   CIP

British Library Cataloging in Publication Data available

Contents

Introduction *Benita J. Howell*	1
Cultural Conservation: Policy and Discipline Implications in a Term *John H. Peterson*	5
Cultural Pluralism and the Conservation of Southern Culture: The New Deal Precedent *Jerrold Hirsch*	20
History and Much, Much More: Historic and Cultural Conservation in Vicksburg, Mississippi *Ralph J. Bishop and Nancy H. Bell*	34
Writing Popular History: Contrasting Approaches from Rural Mississippi and Rural Canada *Seena B. Kohl*	42
New Ways for Old: Assessing Contributions of the Tennessee Community Heritage Project *Betty J. Duggan*	54
The Past and the Present: Urban Archaeology in Charleston, South Carolina *Martha A. Zierden*	66
Appalshop: Preserving, Participating in, and Creating Southern Mountain Culture *Helen M. Lewis*	79

Catface Country: A Case Study in Cultural Conservation 87
Roger G. Branch and Richard Persico, Jr.

Heritage Conservation and Public Education:
The Ozarks Elementary Curriculum Project 96
William Wedenoja and Russel L. Gerlach

Cherokee Sacred Sites in the Appalachians 107
Barbara L. Reimensnyder

Cultural Conservation and Government Planning 118
Carl Fleischhauer

Appalachian Tourism and Cultural Conservation 125
Benita J. Howell

Contributors 141

Cultural Heritage Conservation
in the American South

Introduction

Benita J. Howell

The papers collected in this volume were originally presented at the 1988 Southern Anthropological Society meeting in Tampa, Florida, as the key symposium entitled "Cultural Conservation in the American South: Preserving Our Community Heritage." I appreciate the interest and support of John Peterson, who suggested that I organize a symposium on this topic, and of the Southern Anthropological Society officers, who made their key symposium available as a forum for social scientists trained in history, geography, sociology, folklore, anthropology, and archaeology to discuss an emerging field of common concern.

The term "cultural conservation" was coined to encompass the varied goals of historic preservation, local and regional history, and folklife programs. These endeavors share a fundamental concern with heritage preservation but also with maintenance of living expressions of traditional culture. While effective protection for architectural and archaeological resources is firmly established in federal policy, other manifestations of cultural heritage have not achieved comparable recognition in legislation and agency regulations. Acknowledging the need for a more comprehensive approach to cultural heritage, Congress in the 1980 amendments to the National Historic Preservation Act (Title 3, Section 502) commissioned the Secretary of the Interior, in cooperation with the American Folklife Center of the Library of Congress, to prepare a report on "preserving and conserving the intangible elements of our cultural heritage such as arts, skills, folklife, and folkways," and to recommend federal legislative and administrative actions "in order to preserve, conserve, and encourage the continuation of the diverse traditional prehistoric, historic, ethnic, and folk cultural traditions that underlie and are a living expression of our American heritage."

An interdisciplinary task force was created in response to this Congressional directive. The task force report, *Cultural Conservation: The*

Protection of Cultural Heritage in the United States, was coordinated by Ormond Loomis, director of the Florida Folklife Program, and published by the Library of Congress in 1983. As John Peterson, one of the task force members, describes in the first paper of this volume, the term "cultural conservation" emerged from task force members' efforts to find a mutually satisfactory and politically useful label for their domain of common concern.

The task force recommended expanding the scope of federally mandated historic preservation to encompass encouragement (i.e., conservation) of living cultural traditions but also recognized that cultural conservation would require both public and private efforts at local, state, and national levels. How are the professionals concerned with cultural resources—social scientists in academic institutions and those practicing in museums, historical societies, or government agencies—to approach the task of developing comprehensive, effective programs as recommended in *Cultural Conservation?* How can citizen volunteers best be mobilized to participate in these efforts and support them politically? Contributors to this volume address these and other issues raised by the cultural conservation imperative, drawing on their experiences in diverse research, education, and citizen-action projects organized with and for participants of all ages.

My primary goal in organizing this symposium was to increase familiarity with the term "cultural conservation"—a new label for a range of related interests shared by anthropology and many sister disciplines. Contributions were chosen to illustrate the range of projects and activities which might appropriately be labelled with this new term, and to recognize the work of pioneers who were busy preserving and perpetuating Southern traditions long before "cultural conservation" became a federal policy issue. The South's heightened historical awareness, traditional agrarian values, and distinctive racial-ethnic mix seem to have instilled a natural preoccupation with cultural heritage and stimulated a vast array of projects which fit the current definition of cultural conservation.

The papers in this volume reflect the diversity of disciplines and organizations which might be mobilized in a comprehensive national cultural conservation effort. The authors represent the disciplines of history, sociology, geography, and folklore, as well as archaeology, ethnology, and applied anthropology. They have worked in federal, state, and community programs as employees of academic institutions, museums, private organizations, and government agencies. Similarly, the localities and groups discussed here represent the diversity of Southern cultural traditions—mountain and lowland, rural and urban, Afro-American, Indian, WASP, and ethnic.

Two recurrent themes unite the papers. The first is the pervasive impact which government, particularly the federal government, has had on our cultural heritage. Sometimes government has threatened traditional cultures in its role as public lands manager and developer, but it has also provided leadership and financial support for conservation, as in the establishment of the Federal Writers Program, the American Folklife Center, and the National Endowments for the Arts and Humanities, whose state councils supported most of the funded projects described here.

The second theme is the importance of grassroots participation, whether by dedicated individuals like Eva Whitaker Davis of Vicksburg, Mississippi, and Denver Hollingsworth of Bulloch County, Georgia, who spearheaded historic preservation in their communities, or by Cherokee elders or southwest Virginians daring to protest the cultural impacts of federal agency decisions. Formally organized projects likewise have attempted to stimulate and broaden grassroots participation in various ways: through the collaborative research model adopted by the Mississippi and Tennessee state humanities programs; through involvement of young people, as in the Charleston Museum's urban archaeology program and the Ozarks Elementary Curriculum Project; or through expression and celebration of cultural identity in mass media forms like Appalshop films and the Catface Country Turpentine Festival.

Bolstered by increasing governmental and community interest, "cultural conservation" is emerging as a well-defined field of scholarly and public-sector effort, yet many philosophical, methodological, and policy issues remain to be addressed. If this volume acquaints readers with the scope of cultural conservation concerns and stimulates some to join in the work ahead, it will have fulfilled its purpose.

NOTE

Special thanks are due the symposium participants, all of whom contributed final versions of their papers to this volume; to series editor Mary Helms; and to Betty Duggan, Joyce Nichols, and Thomas Howell, who helped with preparation of the manuscript.

Cultural Conservation: Policy and Discipline Implications in a Term

John H. Peterson

Academic meaning is developed for any term through discipline-specific publications and presentations. As a result, the academic perspective may overlook critical political processes involved in producing a policy document such as *Cultural Conservation* (Loomis 1983), and fail to see the legislative and public communication functions of a term such as "cultural conservation." This paper examines the process of development of policy terms, which I claim is a necessary prospective for considering the term "cultural conservation."

The basis for this paper lies in my participation as one of seven consultants to the *Cultural Conservation* report and in my experiences on the National Heritage Task Force, as an American Anthropological Association Congressional Fellow, and as chairman of a review panel on Cultural Attributes of Water Resources for the National Academy of Sciences. Other anthropologists share similar experiences, but the discipline-centered reporting of policy experience is rare (Peterson 1978) because such experiences are rarely germane to the theoretical and methodological issues of anthropology. I will begin by reviewing the National Heritage Task Force preceding the *Cultural Conservation* report, to demonstrate the normative patterns involved in the development of policy documents.

THE NATIONAL HERITAGE TRUST TASK FORCE

On May 23, 1977, President Carter directed the Secretary of the Interior to develop a National Heritage Trust proposal within 120 days. Immediately, a National Heritage Trust Task Force was created within the Department of the Interior. In addition to a small full-time staff, the task force included over one hundred members representing some fifty public agencies and private organizations. Carter's initial message (Prichard 1977a:40) placed an emphasis on "preserving places that have special natural, historical, cultural, and scientific value."

In early meetings, representatives to the task force were organized into committees representing these four major resource areas, including a Cultural Resources Committee. The discipline of anthropology was well represented by archaeologists from agencies, but no cultural anthropologists were present. In 1981, federal agencies involved in "heritage" programs did not employ cultural anthropologists or have concern for the culture of living peoples. In the task force, federal archaeologists argued that cultural heritage should be considered in a broader context than place. They were joined in this view by representatives of the National Endowment for the Arts, the National Endowment for the Humanities, and the Folklife Center of the Library of Congress.

As a result, the Phase One report of the Committee on Cultural Resources (Prichard 1977a:40) recognized four categories of cultural resources: places, objects and collections, arts and skills, and folklife/contemporary cultures. At this point I was asked as a cultural anthropologist to join the Cultural Resources Committee as a representative of the American Anthropological Association.

The purpose of Phase Two was to take the categories developed in Phase One and identify the goals, objectives, and protection/implementation options for each category. In Phase Two, individuals from each agency and discipline served on different subcommittees working on specific areas under the four major committees. Working on the Folklife/Contemporary Cultures Subcommittee, I offered language relating to social impact of developmental projects on human communities. Folklorists on the subcommittee contributed information on programs and legislation on folklore. Others made similar contributions on programs and legislation in their own policy areas resulting in a statement of goals and objectives, existing programs, and unmet needs. Each subcommittee report, with some reworking, became part of the Phase Two report (Prichard 1977b).

This effort illustrates the professional discipline and governmental agency conflict which surrounds the formation of policy documents. For example, the designation of "arts and skills" as one category and "folklife/contemporary cultures" as another were compromise decisions. Folklorists did not want to have folk skills separated from folklife; they questioned whether by association with arts, they would be overshadowed by the fine arts. But too much effort had been invested in establishing the Folk Arts Program within the National Endowment for the Arts that same year (Loomis 1983:104–105) for the representatives of folk art to be willing to concede a category for the arts without also including folk arts. By using the title "arts and skills" the category of art included folk art and folk skills. Thus the subcommittee title "arts and skills" and report represented a compromise perspective of the fine arts and the advocates of folk art and folklife.

Anthropologists tended to dislike the term "folklife" because it sounded too much like folklore and because such a term might imply only more traditional ways of life. Folklorists responded that this was the very stereotype which they were trying to overcome. Anthropologists preferred the word "culture" but folklorists suggested this word was vague and had diverse meanings including the "high" culture of arts and music, which was already in another subcommittee. The use of a title "folklife/contemporary cultures" represented a discipline and agency compromise on this point between folklore and anthropology. Lacking an acceptable common word, two terms were used separated by a slash implying their equivalent meaning. Any policy study or proposal will reflect similar compromises, often from strongly defended positions, which must be resolved quickly so that parties to the dispute can work together to defend their compromise against other interests working at different levels in the decision-making process. Such compromises represent a complex interplay of academic disciplines, bureaucratic turf, and past legislative and administrative history. Academics are well aware of discipline factors, but are less concerned with or knowledgeable about bureaucratic turf or legislative and administrative history (except in their own departments or universities). As a Congressional Fellow in 1977–1978, I participated in many meetings between Congressional staff members in which compromise wording was negotiated. Never were individuals working on compromise language interested in academic discipline realities, except where these were reflected in bureaucratic turf.

Regardless of their academic discipline, individuals employed by federal agencies or on Congressional staffs react primarily in terms of bureaucratic turf and legislative/administrative history in choice of policy terminology. Constituencies to be served are a related factor. There is a practical recognition that whatever the resulting document, it will be reviewed at the next level by individuals with little or no concern for discipline implications but with primary concern for practical politics. In the case of the Heritage Task Force Report, committee reports were reviewed by the Task Force Director, whose background was in outdoor recreation management, then by the Secretary of the Interior, then by the Office of Management and Budget, and then by the President. Once our report left the Committee on Cultural Resources, it was never seen by a person with academic discipline expertise in "cultural resources." Policy language must be meaningful to governmental officials, legislators, and ultimately to the general public. Academic discipline meaning is unimportant.

Participation in policy efforts demands a willingness to compromise to achieve the best team product. One must accept the limitations of the situation and provide the best possible input under the circumstances. For example, most of the folklorists were interested in both folk skills and folklife. They did not approve of the separation of these two terms in the Phase One report or in the structure of the Phase Two meetings. But when this decision was made, they split between the two subcommittees to ensure that folklore interests were represented in both. One folklorist, going to the Arts and Skills subcommittee, said: "Someone with a folklore background has got to make sure that bunch doesn't become too arty." At one level, folklorists and archaeologists (acting as anthropologists) cooperated against what they saw as the elitism of the arts, art historians, and architectural historians. Folklorists and anthropologists were also united in their efforts to achieve a place in the Heritage report for intangibles such as folk skills, folklife, and culture. At another level, each discipline and agency acted first in its own interests, but there were exceptions. An archaeologist, Dee Green, served as chairman of the subcommittee on Folklife/Contemporary Cultures, because he saw the need for continuity in this subcommittee. He knew that archaeology was already represented in other subcommittees. To maintain credibility, people must be flexible, contribute to the overall effort, and fight only for the most critical points.

Green's participation in this key role illustrates another major point: the importance of having anthropologists present in agencies. Green was able to play a major role because his agency assigned him to work on the task force. Academic anthropologists have difficulty getting away from teaching assignments for concentrated blocks of time. Agency anthropologists are better able to determine when a policy issue may be worthy of following up. The effort to expand the concept of cultural resources came primarily from federal employees, not only in archaeology, but also in folklore, the humanities, and the arts. Academic anthropologists could only help with this effort after the initial direction had been established.

The 1977 effort to expand the concept of cultural resources failed because of the lack of a clear mandate in existing legislation (legislative history), the lack of significant interest by established agencies (bureaucratic turf), and the absence of significant support from publics interested in the preservation of living cultural resources. Policy change requires expert input at the critical point of decision-making, backed by significant, vocal constituencies. Anthropological expertise, even coupled with knowledge of the policy-making process, carries limited weight in effecting policy change without active support from recognized and continuing significant constituencies. Such alignment of constituencies and professional disciplines has been established in varying degrees in archaeology, folklife, and historical preservation. Cultural anthropology as a discipline (or sub-discipline) lacks the unified constituency of these other fields and has many different topics and subjects of study, making a focused approach to policy almost impossible. In my opinion, cultural anthropologists can be more effective in most policy areas through coalitions with other disciplines and groups, rather than by trying to create an anthropological policy position.

THE CULTURAL CONSERVATION REPORT

The next major effort to expand the concept of culture resources originated in the National Historic Preservation Act Amendments of 1980 described in the Introduction to this volume. The House of Representatives report on Section 502 clearly stated the aims of the legislation. The "intangible elements" of our national heritage need to be "identified and afforded appropriate protection and benefits, such as those protections now accorded tangible historical resources" (United

Table 1
Comparison of Policy Language

	Policy Area		Enumeration		Action
National Heritage Task Force of 1977	intangible elements of our cultural heritage	such as	arts skills folklife folkways	should be	preserved conserved
Historical Preservation Act of 1980	intangible living cultural traditions	such as	prehistoric historic ethnic folk	should be	preserved conserved encouraged

States House of Representatives 1980). It is instructive to compare the Cultural Resources subcommittees (and categories) of the 1977 Heritage Task Force with the key sentences of the 1980 legislation, as shown in Table 1.

Since "cultural intangibles" ultimately were eliminated from the Heritage Task Force Report, the 1980 Congressional mandate was to determine the legislative precedents and practical reasons for granting some degree of protection to these "intangibles." Thus, the 1980 legislation identifies as an area of concern precisely those intangible cultural traditions which were rejected from the Heritage Task Force Report. This is an example of administrative/legislative history, or, in different words, an example of the public policy process. Similarity of language does not necessarily reflect direct borrowing from previous policy efforts. It can be a similar response to the same pressures of bureaucratic turf, administrative and legislative history, and constituencies available for potential support.

In the 1980 legislation "contemporary" has been dropped from "culture" and "culture" now appears in connection with two new words "cultural heritage" and "cultural traditions." The area of concern is not preservation of all aspects of "contemporary culture," but only of those aspects which represent part of our "cultural heritage" of our "living cultural traditions." The authors of this legislation also realized that the word "culture" used alone is so broad as to be virtually meaningless. Hence they chose to refer to our "cultural heritage" and to "living cultural traditions." To ensure the scope of meaning was understood, both key sentences in the legislation were followed by lists. The first list identified different elements of a cultural heritage, while the second identified different cultural traditions.

The argument as to how one could draw a line between all contemporary cultures and those reflecting our "living cultural traditions" was a major battle during the preparation of the Cultural Conservation Report. It is impossible to place an equal value on conserving everything. Here the alternative list in the second sentence comes into play. "Living cultural traditions" should be preserved, conserved, and encouraged when they represent prehistoric, historic, ethnic, or folk traditions. This example also illustrates another difference between policy terms and discipline terms. Policy terms evolve around public issues which ultimately reflect action to be taken or prevented. Practical needs stated in general language become policy terms. Academic discipline terms are more likely to be discipline specific language resulting from specialized needs within a field, perhaps with practical consequences within the discipline, but rarely aimed at practical actions for the general public, administrators, or legislators.

Significant in both lists are the words "folk," "folklife," and "folkways." As noted previously, anthropologists do not tend to use these words and identify them with the discipline of folklore. On the other hand, from a folklore perspective, much of the verbiage in the legislation is unnecessary, since the word "folklife" is exactly what is being considered and this term is legally defined in the American Folklife Preservation Act of 1976. For the general public, the terms "folk" and "folklife" may seem to be restricted to certain social groups or settings, and therefore "folk" and "folklife" would not be inclusive of all elements of the American heritage. Folklorists constantly try to educate the public (including anthropologists) that folklife includes both contemporary and traditional cultural patterns of all groups. But they are no more successful in getting general acceptance of their meaning of "folklife" than anthropologists are in getting general acceptance of an anthropological definition of culture. The language of the legislation avoids taking sides in this academic dispute by using both words "culture" and "folk."

The wording in the legislation skillfully covers other quite diverse audiences and constituencies. The use of the fourfold enumeration of living cultural traditions (prehistoric, historic, ethnic, and folk) is unnecessary for cultural anthropologists or folklorists, but it attempts to be exhaustive in appealing to every variety of living cultural tradition. Beyond this, there is a broad appeal to constituent groups and professions which identify with the words "historic," "heritage," and "traditions." This language is more in keeping with the interests of state and local historical societies and other groups which tend to emphasize "high" culture, or "mainstream" American traditions as opposed to anthropologists, folklorists, and ethnic/racial groups which tend to be more interested in cultural diversity and non-WASP traditions. In this regard, the language of the 1980 legislation is more restrictive than the broader term "folklife/contemporary cultures" in the Heritage Task Force Report. At the same time it appeals to a much broader constituency of "heritage" interests and organizations who would be less interested in "folklife" or "contemporary culture."

Thus in two short sentences, the Congressional legislation establishes an appeal which is broader than any of the professional disciplines involved in historical preservation and which also is inclusive of all the potential living cultural traditions within the United States. Any member of Congress could say that all of the peoples in his district were covered by this Congressional concern. This breadth is achieved by using a variety of words which appeal to different professional and public constituencies. There is not a superfluous word nor is there a technical word in either sentence.

But what can this effort be called? The distinguishing feature of Section 502 was its focus on the "intangible." The only other possible general term, "folklife," is identified with the American Folklife Center and with the discipline of folklore. "Intangible" was a new word not associated with any discipline, bureaucracy, or established constituency. Hence, informal references were made to an "intangible study" which was presumably to lead to the "intangible report." Since there was no active constituency group pushing for this study, and since the Reagan administration was uninterested in policy initiatives in this area, there was a bit of black humor involved in the term "intangible study."

The procedures for the "intangible study" were quite different from the National Heritage Task Force. The mandate for the study came from Congress, not the President. Thus there was no immediate administrative directive from the Secretary of the Interior to create a task force. The Congressional legislation directed the Secretary of the Interior to undertake the report in cooperation with the American Folklife Center of the Library of Congress. This direction recognized a major reality: the location of professional staff in Washington, D.C., with expertise required to oversee and administer the study. The implementation of the Historic Preservation Act lies with the Department of the Interior, which was well staffed with archaeologists; but because there was then no clear mandate for protection of intangible cultural resources, the department did not have professional staff in this area.

To ensure that such views were represented, it seemed desirable to bring into the study, through language in the legislation, a professional group within the national government with interests in preservation of cultural intangibles. The alternatives were the folklife programs within the National Endowment for the Arts, the Office of Folklife Programs in the Smithsonian Institution, and the American Folklife Center of the Library of Congress. The first two of these programs are located in independent agencies and entities, while the Library of Congress is officially part of Congress and serves in direct support of the legislative efforts of Congress. Bennie C. Keel, then Departmental Consulting Archaeologist of the Department of the Interior, and Alan Jabbour, Director of the American Folklife Center, were personally committed to the concept of the study and were both in a position to recommend resources for carrying out of the study. Under the mandate of the legislation, these two agencies executed a memorandum of agreement under which they shared the costs and direction of the project (Loomis 1983:81). Keel and Jabbour remained jointly responsible for the project and report until shortly before completion of the final draft on July 15, 1982.

Thus rather than a broad multi-agency task force ordered by the President, the "cultural intangible" study proceeded with a small agreement between Interior and the Library of Congress, and a single study director hired for one year, Ormond Loomis, a folklorist from the Florida Folklife Program. Agency input began with an initial one-day meeting of agency personnel and private organizations held on November 17, 1981. This was followed by a two-day meeting of a seven-person consultant team on November 19 and 20, 1981. This team was appointed to guide report preparation and serve as a balance between the two agencies and diverse interests. The consultants were all non-agency persons, but each had extensive experience in one or more aspects of preservation of cultural resources, tangible and intangible. The team included the following persons and specializations:

Steven Arvizu, cultural anthropology, bilingual/bicultural programs, Advisory Council on Historical Preservation
James Deetz, historical archaeology, museums, anthropology, folklore
Henry Glassie, folklore, folk architecture, state folklorist
Archie Green, folklore, folklore legislation including formation of the American Folklife Center
Ruthann Knudson, anthropological archaeology, archaeology legislation including 1980 Historical Preservation Act
John Peterson, cultural anthropologist, environmental impacts, Congressional experience
Robert Stipe, state historical preservation officer, preservation law, Executive Board of the National Trust for Historical Preservation

Present at all consultant team meetings were Keel and Jabbour, and the study director, Loomis.

The federal agency representatives and the consultants agreed that there was a need to broaden the concept of cultural resources to include cultural intangibles, but that there was little possibility of securing significant new legislation in 1981. Rather, the effort should be to broaden the concept of cultural resources to include cultural intangibles in appropriate existing legislation and regulations. The consultants agreed that the major thrust of the "cultural intangibles" study would be to document the degree to which a concern for cultural intangibles was growing in federal legislation, and the variety of exemplary efforts being made in the private and public sectors.

One month after the first meeting to set the direction for the study, the consultant group met again in Washington to develop a detailed outline for the report. The consultants identified outstanding examples of cultural intangibles projects and returned home to begin assisting in study documentation. From December until March, the study director gathered additional material and prepared a preliminary statement of findings and recommendations which were shared with the consultant team and all interested parties. The study director and members of the consultant team also presented the preliminary recommendations to the annual meetings of the National Conference of State Historical Preservation Officers and the Society for Applied Anthropology. On March 15 and 16, the consultant team reconvened in Washington to discuss the draft report, which was revised and further reviewed by mail, resulting in the completed report.

It is impossible to review the contents of the report in this article. It is the best available review of related legislation and examples of local, state, and federal initiatives to preserve intangible cultural resources. The papers in this volume will give a flavor of the activities which the *Cultural Conservation* report attempts to promote. The participants in the cultural intangibles study had no illusions that we would be making a decisive and definitive effort on behalf of preservation of cultural intangibles. We hoped that we could document a growing concern for extending preservation protection from tangible properties to include the people and their activities.

But what to call this effort? "Cultural intangibles" was a "fun" reference term, but it was impossible as a public policy term or as a discipline term. The report, *Cultural Conservation*, uses a variety of words and phrases to express a sense of what was to be preserved. The opening section (Loomis 1983:27) under the title "Cultural Conservation" states: "This study addresses community life and values—folklife." Other words used in this section come from the study mandate ("intangible elements of our cultural heritage") and from historical preservation legislation ("cultural resources").

The seven-person consultant team fought as strongly among ourselves over the alternative meanings of "folklife," "culture," "traditional cultures," and all the variants as had the Heritage Task Force four years previously. But we had two advantages. As a smaller group, our disagreements could be based on a clear understanding of each other's positions. Secondly, since none of the consultants was based in any specific agency, we were concerned only with the goal of preserving cultural intangibles and how the report could promote this goal. We found it impossible to agree on a term which expressed exactly what we mean by cultural intangibles. I believe the two sentences in the Congressional legislation form the best definition of what we wish to preserve, conserve, and encourage.

But in the midst of our arguing, we did manage to hit upon a term to call what we were all interested in promoting. We were interested in preserving, conserving, encouraging a continuation of the cultural diversity which makes up the American heritage. Preserving sounds too much like making pickles and putting them on the shelf (Alan Jabbour, personal communication, 1981). Encouraging cultural diversity reaches far beyond current goals and has too many political implications. "Conserving culture" seemed to express the goals we shared. "Conserving" implies not just preserving a lifeless artifact, but encouraging a living cultural pattern to continue to exist. We were talking about "Cultural Conservation," a term which parallels "Historic Preservation" but encourages an appreciation for and maintenance of the culture of living people. Or if you prefer, "Cultural Conservation" involves the conservation of folklife. There is always a danger in attempting to recommend a new term. But it seemed inappropriate to try to expand the excellent term "historic preservation" beyond its current boundaries. The only other term existing in legislation is "folklife," but this term has liabilities in being associated with a specific academic discipline. So the term "cultural conservation" was the unanimous selection of the consultant team, the study director, and the two agency representatives. But what was to be the scope of cultural conservation? The consultant team finally agreed on six primary activities:

1. Planning carefully in the development of projects to avoid unnecessary disruption of traditional community patterns;
2. Documenting vanishing forms of expression to create a record of valuable attributes subject to unavoidable disruption;
3. Maintenance of endangered skills and activities to extend their life;
4. Publication of books, records, and films to disseminate information about distinctive cultural features;
5. Public events providing live presentation of traditional activities; and
6. Educational programs about significant cultural traditions to promote an appreciation for the wealth of diverse cultural resources in the United States.

There were extended arguments about each of these activities, their relative importance, and the need to stress other activities. There were arguments about almost everything else in the report, except the overall goal. Loomis did an outstanding job of listening to all the arguments and recommendations, reading all the red-lined drafts returned to him, and coming up with a report which coherently reflects the consultants' consensus, as well as the input from agency personnel and others.

While the final draft report was being completed, a reorganization in the Department of the Interior led to the transfer of authority for the report within the department. Subsequently, and for reasons not identified, the Department of the Interior withdrew from sponsorship of the report which subsequently appeared as a publication of the American Folklife Center. Unfortunately, the withdrawal of Interior sponsorship gave the appearance that the report was produced solely by the American Folklife Center and thus represented the position of an agency concerned with folklife and associated with the discipline of folklore (Kealinohomoku 1987; Peterson 1987). As this article has stated, the study was jointly directed from the beginning, and the consultant team was evenly balanced between folklorists and anthropologists. Although the study director was a folklorist, whenever there was disagreement over wording, he accepted all suggestions agreed upon by the anthropologists.

It is most significant that although the Department of the Interior withdrew from joint issuing of the report, it is the Department of the Interior, especially the National Park Service (Crespi 1987), which has made the greatest strides to implement the activities of Cultural Conservation, often specifically using this term. The National Park Service has hired personnel with ethnographic skills to carry out activities related to living cultural traditions (folklife) at the national and the individual park level (Brassieur 1987). Cultural Conservation is becoming a term with real meaning in some federal agencies.

In conclusion, I believe that "Cultural Conservation" is the best policy term for what we are advocating. I am convinced that "folklife" is a better policy term for what we are trying to conserve than is the broader term "culture" or any other equivalent anthropological term. Folklife has the added advantage of already being defined in law.

I am also convinced that until we can stop defending discipline turf and discipline terms and come together to articulate a public policy we can all support, we will have no policy, few programs, and little protection for the people and cultures which deserve better from us than self-serving academic squabbles.

Cultural anthropologists interested in the work presented in this volume under the term "Cultural Conservation" may find that their closest allies and collaborators lie outside their discipline in neighboring disciplines which share interests in historic preservation, folklife, folk art, and public programming in art, humanities, and folklore. Who knows, perhaps even archaeologists and cultural anthropologists will find commonalities for parallel work in cultural resources management and cultural conservation. Further developments in Cultural Conservation require efforts at consensus building between professional disciplines and between professionals and the publics they serve. Cultural Conservation is also promoted by scholarly exchange in interdisciplinary symposia such as this. "Cultural Conservation" is a new term. Good or bad, strong or weak, it will represent as much or as little as we make it represent.

REFERENCES

American Folklife Preservation Act, 1976. Public Law 94–201, 86 Stat. 1129, 20 U.S. Code 2101.
Brassieur, C. Ray, 1987. An Overview of Ethnographic Studies Sponsored by Jean Lafitte National Historical Park. Paper presented at the Information Transfer Meeting for Environmental Studies, Minerals Management Service, U.S. Department of the Interior, New Orleans, December 1–3, 1987.
Crespi, Muriel, 1987. Ethnography and the NPS. *Cultural Resources Management Bulletin* 10(1):1–4.
Kealinohomoku, Joann W., 1987. Holistic Culture, Resource Management. *Practicing Anthropology* 9(4):2,18–19.
Loomis, Ormond, H., coordinator, 1983. *Cultural Conservation: The Protection of Cultural Heritage in the United States* (Washington, D.C.: Library of Congress).
Peterson, John H., 1978. Public Policy Processes: Implications for Applied Anthropology. In *Anthropology for the Future*, Demitri B. Shimkin, Sol Tax, and John W. Morrison, eds. (Urbana: University of Illinois), pp. 204–210.
——— , 1987. Reply to Holistic Culture, Resource Management. *Practicing Anthropology* 9(4):18–19.

Prichard, Paul C., 1977a. Phase One Report of the National Heritage Task Force, July 25. (Washington, D.C.: U.S. Department of the Interior).
———, 1977b. Phase Two Report of the National Heritage Task Force, August 23. (Washington, D.C.: U.S. Department of the Interior).
United States House of Representatives, 1980. Report No. 96–1457, Title 3, Section 502.

Cultural Pluralism and the Conservation of Southern Culture: The New Deal Precedent

Jerrold Hirsch

It would be both ironic and tragic if those interested in cultural conservation failed to assess and learn from previous efforts in this area. Indefatigable researchers are working hard to retrieve the cultural studies of the New Deal's Federal Writers' Project (FWP) and to assess their value for studying American culture—yet much still remains to be done. The FWP's Southern studies were among its most innovative and important efforts at cultural conservation—life histories of Southern tenant farmers, interviews with former slaves, and folklore studies in addition to the guidebooks to the Southern states in the American Guide Series.[1] Scholars, however, are so busy using these materials (after some hesitation) that crucial points are in danger of being lost. National FWP officials wanted their studies to reach a general audience and to influence American art and thought. They thought their efforts at cultural conservation would contribute to the embracing of American cultural pluralism as a basis for a form of national integration that was inclusive, not exclusive, and democratic, not coercive. FWP officials had a vision of the role of cultural conservation (although it is unlikely they used that term) in a democratic society and their goals are worth studying as an episode in American cultural and intellectual history and as part of the New Deal program of political and economic reform (see Hirsch 1984, 1988). Understanding their visions can help us develop and clarify our own assumptions and visions.

The FWP, with its national officials and regional and state directors, had a regional and local as well as a national point of view. It brought together within a national framework individuals from all points on a local-national continuum. The dialogue that resulted was a product of circumstances, not choice. It was a community held together by its members' relationship to the Writers' Project. In this paper I intend to focus on the aims and hopes of those who worked on the FWP Southern studies and the conflicts that sometimes developed between local FWP project writers, state directors, and national officials. These conflicts illustrate differing attitudes toward the Southern past, present, and future—different visions of Southern and national problems and goals. The FWP's treatment of Southern studies needs to be examined in the context of long standing debates about Southern identity and culture and the region's relation to the rest of the nation. The dialogue between national FWP officials and Southern FWP writers illuminates not only an attempt to encourage the documentation of intangible elements of cultural heritage, but also a debate about the political and cultural implications of the conservation of diverse regional traditions.

The work of the FWP in the South can help remind us that the question of what deserves celebration as regional heritage is potentially controversial. While it is important to consider current criticism about the consensual and celebratory nature of cultural conservation programs that claim to be apolitical, but in fact endorse the status quo (see Kirshenblatt-Gimblett 1988:142), it is also important to remember that there are times when the act of celebration is itself a challenge to the status quo. In some ways, the discussion among FWP writers about how to publically present Southern traditions can be viewed as an example of that critical discourse regarding the political implications of cultural conservation which is deeply needed but too often does not take place.

In the New Deal's program for economic recovery and reform the South loomed large (see Tindall 1967; Freidel 1965). The New Deal cultural projects complemented the thrust of its social and economic programs, and here, too, the South was a significant concern. True, the administration invested only limited political capital in its cultural projects. In the Southern FWP units the possibility that parochialism would prevent the development of what national FWP officials considered a healthy provincialism compatible with a cosmopolitan outlook was greater and clearer than anywhere else in the nation. In the South, as in the rest of the nation, but most starkly in the former Confederacy, attitudes toward the Negro provided the ultimate answer as to how the majority defined democracy, equality, community, and American national identity. These issues were at the heart of the FWP dialogue between members of a nationally oriented, left of center, cosmopolitan, and ethnically diverse intellectual community, and locally oriented, often conservative, and predominantly white Southerners involved in producing the state guidebooks (Hirsch 1984:382–424).

Equally important, however, were two other discussions. W. T. Couch, southeast regional FWP director and head of the University of North Carolina Press, was at the center of one of those discussions. Couch directed a Southern life history program that collected over a thousand interviews with ordinary Southerners, black and white (Terrill and Hirsch 1978; Hirsch 1984:395–423). The other discussion involved Southern FWP writers, national FWP officials, and former slaves, and produced a collection of ex-slave narratives, whose publication in 1972 historian David Brion Davis has called one of the major turning points in the post–World War II historiography of slavery (Davis 1974:2).

An examination of the discussion within the FWP about the Southern guidebooks, the Southern life history program, and the ex-slave interviews makes it possible to look at various ways in which cultural conservation programs address questions about the past, present, and future. In moving from an examination of the Southern guidebooks to an analysis of W. T. Couch's Southern life history program the discussion proceeds from a description of dominant white Southern middle-class attitudes to an analysis of the attitudes of a white Southern liberal intellectual. Perhaps it is inevitable that I end with the dialogue about including the voices of former slaves in the presentation of Southern cultural traditions, for the politics of cultural representation can reflect the central tensions of a social order.

National FWP officials tried to conduct studies of American culture that would broaden the definition of who and what was American. These studies celebrated a pluralistic culture. The dialogue that took place between Southern FWP writers and national FWP officials in the course of writing guidebooks has something to say concerning white middle-class Southern attitudes toward the changes resulting from the transition from an agrarian to an industrial society. While industrialism and urbanism did not become a majority way of life for Southerners until after World War II, perceptions that this was the way Southern society was moving date back to Henry Grady, who in the late nineteenth century popularized the idea of a New South. The New Deal, with its Tennessee Valley Authority, Rural Electrification Act, Agricultural Adjustment Act, and a host of other programs that affected Southern agriculture and industry, reinforced (as the guidebooks illustrate), the idea that Southern society was about to undergo momentous changes. In the guides, Southern FWP writers indicated that their attitudes toward modern society were intimately tied to their attitude about what time and space had meant in the Southern way of life and that these attitudes were tightly bound up with their view of race relations (cf. Hirsch 1986:xi–lv).

National officials wanted Southern guides that reflected a vision compatible with their own. None of the Southern guides identified a rejection of industrialism as the touchstone of loyalty to the Southern tradition. In that sense, none embodied what national folklore editor B. A. Botkin had called the Southern Agrarians' "mistake of identifying culture with a particular trait or complex, a particular way of life . . . of taking a certain background for granted, and a certain social order as final" (Botkin 1937:141). The Southern FWP writers did, however, take the Negro's place in Southern life for granted, as final, and as central to their idea of the South. They lived in a dual society. Unlike national FWP officials they did not envision a pluralist culture based on relativistic and egalitarian values. Few would have understood or agreed with Botkin's argument that "cultural minorities and other non-dominant groups . . . were not static but dynamic and transitional, on their way up" (Botkin 1938:126). At most the Southern members of the Writers' Project envisioned a separate New Deal for blacks.

Sterling Brown, black poet and national FWP Negro affairs editor, worked to see that blacks received adequate treatment in the guides. For the most part, he was working with white Southerners. The number of blacks on each of the Southern state projects could be counted on one hand. The exceptions were Virginia, Louisiana, and Florida which had separate black units (Penkower 1977:66–67). What Brown called stereotypes, Southern FWP writers thought of as knowledge. While he thought FWP studies might reopen questions about the Southern Negro, the white writers wanted them to remain closed. Much of Brown's time was spent deleting stereotypical material from state guide copy sent to Washington and demanding that what he saw as pertinent facts be included (Hirsch 1984:42–50, 535–541). The draft of the local guide to

Beaufort, South Carolina, for example, described Negroes as "a picturesque group," "a happy people, primitive, unmoral," who "for all their seventy odd years of freedom. . . . have never really learned to stand alone" (Federal Writers' Project 193[7?]; Hirsch 1984:387–388)

Here was a test of national FWP officials' desire to reconcile provincialism and cosmopolitanism. For them cosmopolitanism meant a recognition that no one tradition had a complete knowledge of the value and meaning of life; therefore, knowledge of other traditions would broaden one's own perspective. Being provincial was not, in their opinion, incompatible with trying to learn about other traditions (see Hollinger 1975:133–151). They found support for the idea that provincialism and cosmopolitanism were compatible in the work of anthropologist Franz Boas and his students (see Stocking 1968:64–90, 195–233; Hirsch 1984). Boasian anthropology, with its emphasis on the plurality and relativity of historically conditioned cultures, strengthened cosmopolitan ideas among intellectuals. National officials objected to parochialism, the inability or unwillingness to look beyond one's own tradition. The Southern FWP writers, for the most part, lacked any belief in cultural relativity: "When I am asked to tell what the negro has contributed to the culture in such different cities as Winston-Salem and Elizabeth City," Edwin Bjorkman, North Carolina FWP director, declared, "I feel something like despair. In one of these cities you hardly see him . . . in the other you see him only too frequently, but that is all that can be said about him" (Bjorkman 1937). Bjorkman thought of culture in artistic, not anthropological terms, and of art as high culture. This was a point of view national FWP officials rejected since they thought of culture as a way of life, not only as artistic creations, saw cultures in relative terms, and found much to admire in art outside of the western tradition of high culture.

The difference between national FWP officials' vision of America and that of project workers in the South was only occasionally stated in theoretical terms. The Georgia FWP writers who worked on *Drums and Shadows: Survival Studies Among the Georgia Coastal Negroes* (Georgia Writers' Project 1940) did not see their search for African survivals as simply part of the argument about whether American Negroes had a cultural heritage and identity with visible African roots. Rather, they placed the issue of survivals in the context of an evolutionary theory of culture. They thought of culture as a series of stages in a progressive human development. Cultural materials from an earlier and inferior stage might survive, but with progress they would disappear. They linked these ideas to a view of individual psychology as having a biologically and racially determined character. Georgia FWP writers claimed that it was to the primitive, "the survival type," that one had to turn as a source of folklore (FWP n.d.). The evolutionary view precluded any recognition of cultural relativity, any sense that acculturation, change, and adaptation were a two-way exchange, any acknowledgment that folklore was in part a product of the creative and functional response of a culture to a new situation. In short, Georgia FWP writers were in total disagreement with national FWP officials. *Drums and Shadows* (Georgia Writers' Project 1940) was published, but with almost all the narrative and analysis removed.

The Georgia FWP attitude toward African survivals is only one example of the Southern guides' treatment of the Negro from a distance, from the outside. The Southern guides almost always discuss the Negro in the third person. The use of "they" for Negroes always implies that the writer, and other white residents of the region, are *the* Southerners. Thus there are Alabamians and the Alabama Negro, Beaufort residents and Beaufort Negroes, Tar Heels and North Carolina Negroes. Sterling Brown had plans for an FWP study to be entitled "The Negro as American" (Brown 193[7?]). The logical Southern corollary would have been "The Negro as Southerner." Such a study was never proposed and for an obvious reason. It would have required white Southern FWP workers to broaden the term Southerner to include all the residents of the region, just as national FWP officials wanted to broaden the term American.

In the Southern guides talk of a New South is always linked to attitudes about the Old South and the Negro. For these are the terms which have characterized much of the Southern discussion about tradition and modernization. The Alabama guide informs the reader that "the ante bellum mansion and the towering steel mill still symbolize Alabama's dual personality" (FWP 1941a:8). Cotton is an important part of the image, but it is not essential. The Southern guides create dichotomous images through the use of contrasting word-pictures. In Florence, Alabama, "life continues to move easily despite industrial activity initiated by the Tennessee Valley Authority." While "khaki-clad Government engineers move briskly," the local "citizens pause on the courthouse lawn to escape the hot summer sun and to discuss politics, and the well-filled knife-marked benches under the trees may be thought of as symbols of this leisurely city" (FWP 1941a:184). Contrasting images of the Old and New South, of tradition and modernity, are created through the repeated use of such opposite adjectives as drowsy and swift. The change from an agrarian to an industrial South is noted in these adjectives which reflect a sense that traditional notions about time and space have changed. All the adjectives associated with traditional notions and with the Old South, are, however, used to describe the Negro.

The portrait of the Negro in the Southern landscape is an indispensable part of the Old South/New South dichotomy. The Negro is seen as the major constant in Southern history. As long as the contemporary Negro is visible in his traditional roles, Southern guidebook writers can, despite dramatic changes in other aspects of Southern life, assert that white Southerners are still loyal to Southern traditions. According to the Louisiana guide: "While Monroe is [an] essentially modern and semi-urban [city] in aspect, its people cherish many old southern traditions, especially as regards relations between whites and Negroes, hospitality, and a chivalrous attitude toward the ladies" (FWP 1941b:292).

The strong point of all the FWP guides was their portrait of the visible diversity of America. Despite the hopes of national FWP officials that through guidebook tours Americans would discover that what appeared foreign, different, or strange was part of their national identity, the guidebooks also reflected traditional associations between travel and a local color approach to the exploration of folk cultures, between tourist literature and a picturesque emphasis on folk cultures as exotic, quaint, and outlandish (see Fussell 1980:37–50, 57, 62–64, 168, 202–215; Hill 1981:12–29). The guides did not penetrate beneath the visible landscape. Other FWP programs did.

W. T. Couch, FWP southeast regional director, wanted to probe beneath the clichés that rationalized the status quo but did not explain reality. More than most Southerners, Couch shared a similar outlook with national FWP officials. Still his ideas also grew out of an inherited discussion about the South—a discussion in which most national FWP officials were outsiders. Couch's views were not typical of those of most of his fellow white Southerners. He was willing and eager to examine Southern life and problems without paying obeisance to traditional shibboleths. He opposed fellow Southerners who argued "we are held down by the Negro," or "the masses of white people are not particularly hopeful material." He contended the reality was that these ideas only "help keep things as they are" (Couch 1937a). Couch wanted to give ordinary Southerners an opportunity to tell their own story in their own words, to let them participate in longstanding discussions about Southern poverty and the Southern poor.

Couch supervised an extensive FWP program for collecting the life histories of common Southerners. He thought and worked in a cultural context in which the South had become an important symbol of the nation's economic problems. Couch reacted to Southern intellectual developments such as Regionalism and Agrarianism, and to Northern views of Southern problems. He insisted that while the Agrarians rejected industrialism and idealized a simpler agrarian society, their abstractions failed to deal with the realities of Southern life (Hirsch 1984: 395–401). The Agrarians, Couch pointed out, "assert that virtue is derived from the soil, but see no virtue in the Negro and poor white who are closest to the soil" (Couch 1937b:429). Couch's program, however, needs to be understood not only in the context of the thirties, but also in relationship to the discussion he inherited.

Images of poor whites have been with us from William Byrd's colonial description of "Lubberland Land" to Erskine Caldwell's *Tobacco Road* and beyond (McIllwaine 1939; Cook 1976). So, too, have the plain folk and yeoman farmers. The dialogue is as much a battle of counter-images involving the psychological and ideological needs of the participants as it is an attempt to describe reality. The debate is over the character of the subject, and the terms are only vaguely sociological. The same is true for the discussion of black Southerners. Character is ascribed to these individuals either on the basis of a hasty and condescending impressionism or simply on what has been gleaned from other books. Southern mill workers, we are told by one scholar, behave docilely because they have an agrarian background (de Graffenried 1891). Another claims they are fiercely independent for the same reason (McDonald 1928:1944). A Northern reformer contends that diversified farming would make for a less boring lifestyle than cotton culture and thus eliminate behaviors he found repugnant (Tannenbaum 1924:117). Much of this Couch hoped to push aside. And though he blamed the social and economic system rather than these poor individuals for their plight, his program was shaped to a significant extent by an inherited regional dialogue about the character of the Southern poor.

Couch thought in terms of individuals and classes. For the most part he did not think in terms of communities, and hardly at all of communities sharing a folk culture worthy of attention. Despite all that separated his views from those of the average Southern FWP writer, Couch shared with them ways of looking at the South that neither he nor they shared with national FWP officials. Southern FWP writers had a mythic conception of the character of Southern society, past and present, and the proper place of various groups, especially blacks, in that society. The guides offer evidence that much of what they saw as traditional, much that had made them feel secure, they felt was changing in response to modern developments. Couch, however, welcomed many of these changes. Much that his peers did not question he thought merited examination and reform. Nevertheless, he too found himself challenging the character that most middle-class white Southerners attributed to blacks and poor whites. Such notions had behind them a vast body of oral and written tradition. By letting Southerners speak for themselves Couch intended that the actual character of these people would emerge. He, however, was locked into the Southern discussion. He did not move the life histories into an examination of culture.

In contrast, national FWP social-ethnic studies, living lore projects, and black studies used oral interviews to collect folklore and look at culture from a functionalist anthropological perspective (Botkin 1938, 1939, 1940a, 1946, 1958; Hirsch 1984:17–25; 1988). In terms of the politics of culture, such an approach was an assertion that these groups were not simply contributing to American culture, but that their culture was as much American culture as anyone else's. National FWP officials switched the argument over the so-called immigrant problem and race question from a debate about character and heredity to a debate about culture. The Southern life history program did this to a much more limited extent. Though, like national FWP officials, Couch supported liberal social and economic reform, he did not share their relativistic view of culture. And few of the FWP workers who collected the Southern life histories shared Washington's views or Couch's reformist perspective. There is less information about folklife in the Southern life histories than in interviews collected in other FWP projects.

By letting ex-slaves and ordinary Southerners tell their own stories, the FWP allowed people traditionally excluded from public discussions to participate. National FWP officials wanted to reopen the subject of slavery to fresh examination. From the point of view of B. A. Botkin, the national FWP folklore editor who was assigned the task of editing and preparing the ex-slave narratives for publication, both Southern and American identity lay not in a frozen and static tradition, but in the multiple traditions that American folk groups developed and adapted to a changing pluralistic and industrial society (Botkin 1930:16; 1937: 155–156; 1945:xii–xiv). Such a view of Southern identity argued that the voice of the Negro folk experience also had to be heard if black and white Southerners were to understand themselves as both Southerners and Americans. Botkin's *Lay My Burden Down* (1945) could be regarded as a contribution to the task of taking up and recreating a Southern identity that could survive in an increasingly integrated and pluralistic society and contribute to the creation of a democratic national community based on a cosmopolitan awareness of American diversity and a sense of one's own provincial traditions.

Southern FWP writers, with few exceptions, were determined to make the ex-slaves' narratives confirm white Southerners' traditional views of Negroes and slavery. Chalmers S. Murray, South Carolina FWP writer, wrote his state director, "I have thought from the first it was rather a mistake to write these ex-slave stories. . . . The general run of negro is only too glad of an opportunity to record his grievances" (Murray 1937). Scholars have pointed out the challenges in learning how to read and interpret the FWP ex-slave interviews. Some of the exchanges between interviewees and interviewers indicate the ex-slaves viewed the interviewers as individuals who could help them obtain old-age pensions. Many of the ex-slaves resided in the same areas as their masters' descendants and were economically dependent on whites. Most often the interviewers were members of the local white community and sometimes were descendents of the interviewee's former owners. A careful reading of the interviews demonstrates that the former slaves were often guarded in their remarks to white interviewers and tried not to violate the etiquette of race relations that existed in the South in the 1930s. In numerous cases interviewers compulsively strove to have the interviewee confirm their preconceptions about slavery and race relations (Blassingame 1975:473–492; Bailey 1980: 381–404; Hirsch 1980:315–317).

Relations between national FWP officials and local project workers in the South illustrate how radical the idea of a diverse and inclusive community seemed to most white Southerners, and to many other Americans, and still does to some. From the point of view of national FWP officials, such an inclusive community was not meant to buttress social consensus, but to give weight to the claims of such excluded groups as black Americans. Recognizing this, the Southern state Writers' Projects resisted Washington's approach to Southern studies.

Perhaps of all Americans in the thirties, white Southerners found it hardest to attach positive value to the reality of American cultural pluralism. In 1933 when T. S. Eliot told a University of Virginia audience that the South being "farther away from New York" and "less industrialized and less invaded by foreign races" had a better chance "for a reestablishment of a native culture" than any other region, he could assume he had a sympathetic audience for what was not a unique view of tradition and modernity (Eliot 1934:15, 20). In 1935, Texas Representative Martin Dies bemoaned "the great alien invasion" that had destroyed the nation's "racial unity" (Dies 1935). In 1938 the House Un-American Activities Committee, chaired by Martin Dies, used anti-Communist rhetoric to attack the FWP and its pluralistic vision of American culture (Hirsch 1984:214–258). All of this took place at a time when totalitarian societies abroad were forcibly trying to restore a sense of wholeness, a world with one Folk, one Reich, one Führer, and thus offering the allusion of restoring unity to a fragmented nation. In sharp contrast, national FWP officials held that diversity offered hope of cultural renewal. Where Eliot saw only fragmentation and cultural decay, national FWP officials saw pluralism and the opportunity for creating a new revitalized culture and inclusive democratic community based on knowledge of diverse folk traditions.

National FWP officials challenged white Southerners to develop a program of cultural conservation that embodied a vision of their community and a view of their identity and tradition which included blacks as well as whites, the poor as well as the prosperous. Most refused. The Southern FWP writers only partly met the challenge. We have inherited that challenge.

NOTE

1. The entire Federal Writers' Project Southern Life History Collection is available on microfiche from University Microfilms International.

REFERENCES

Bailey, David Thomas, 1980. A Divided Prism: Two Sources of Black Testimony on Slavery. *Journal of Southern Press* 46:381–404.

Bjorkman, Edwin, 1937. Bjorkman to Couch, November 15, 1937. Federal Writers' Project Papers of the Regional Director, William Terry Couch, Southern Historical Collection, University of North Carolina, Chapel Hill, North Carolina, Hereafter referred to as FWP-Couch Papers.

Blassingame, John W., 1975. Using the Testimony of Ex-Slaves: Approaches and Problems. *Journal of Southern History* 41:473–492.

Botkin, B. A., 1930. Introduction. In *Folk-Say, A Regional Miscelany: 1929*, B. A. Botkin, ed. (Norman: University of Oklahoma Press), pp. 15–18.

———, 1937. Regionalism and Culture. In *The Writer in a Changing World*, Henry Hart, ed. (New York: Equinox Press), pp. 140–157.

———, 1938. The Folk and The Individual: Their Creative Reciprocity. *The English Journal* 27:121–135.

———, 1939. WPA and Folklore Research: 'Bread and Song.' *Southern Folklore Quarterly* 3:7–14.

———, 1940a. Folklore as a Neglected Source of Social History. In *The Cultural Approach to History*, Caroline Ware, ed. (New York: Columbia University), pp. 308–315.

———, 1940b. Old and New in New England. In Background of Social-Ethnic Studies, September 18, 1940, Box 210, Federal Writers' Project files, Works Progress Administration, Record Group 69, National Archives, Washington, D.C. Hereafter referred to as FWPNA.

———, ed. 1945. *Lay My Burden Down: A Folk History of Slavery* (Chicago: University of Chicago Press).

———, 1946. Living Lore on the New York City Writers' Project. *New York Folklore Quarterly* 2:252–263.

———, 1958. We Called It 'Living Lore.' *New York Folklore Quarterly* 14:189–198.

Brown, Sterling, 193[7?]. The Portrait of the Negro in America, n.d., Box 210, FWPNA.

Cook, Sylvia Jenkins, 1976. *From Tobacco Road to Route 66: The Southern Poor White in Fiction* (Chapel Hill: University of North Carolina Press).

Couch, W. T., 1937a. Speech at South Georgia Teachers' College, Collegeboro, Georgia, March 12, 193[7?]. FWP-Couch papers.

———, 1937b. The Agrarian Romance. *South Atlantic Quarterly Review* 36:419–430.

Davis, David Brion, 1974. Slavery and Post World War II Historians. *Daedalus* 103(2):1–16.

de Graffenried, Clare, 1891. The Georgia Cracker in the Cotton Mills. *Century* 19:483–498.
Dies, Martin, 1935. Immigration Crisis. *Saturday Evening Post* 207(20 April): 27, 105–106, 108–109, 111–112, 114.
Eliot, T. S., 1934. *After Strange Gods: A Primer of Modern Heresy* (New York: Harcourt, Brace and Company).
Federal Writers' Project, n.d. Draft, Stories of Negro Survival Types in Coastal Georgia. Box 201, FWPNA.
———, 193[7?]. Draft essay on the Negro in Beaufort, South Carolina, n.d. Box 201, Federal Writers' Project files, Works Progress Administration, Record Group 69, National Archives, Washington, D.C.
———, 1941a. *Alabama: A Guide to the Deep South* (New York: Hastings House).
———, 1941b. *Louisiana: A Guide to the State* (New York: Richard R. Smith).
Freidel, Frank, 1965. *FDR and the South* (Baton Rouge: Louisiana State University Press).
Fussell, Paul, 1980. *Abroad: British Literary Traveling Between the Wars* (New York: Oxford University Press).
Georgia Writers' Project, 1940. *Drums and Shadows: Survival Studies Among the Georgian Coastal Negroes*. Reprint, 1986. Introduction by Charles Joyner (Athens: University of Georgia Press).
Hill, Nancy K., 1981. *A Reformer's Art: Dickens' Picturesque and Grotesque Imagery* (Athens: Ohio University Press).
Hirsh, Jerrold, 1980. Reading and Counting. Review of *Slavery Remembered: The Twentieth Century Slave Narratives*. *Reviews in American History* 8: 312–317.
———, 1984. Portrait of America: The Federal Writers' Project in an Intellectual and Cultural Context (Ph.D. diss., University of North Carolina, Chapel Hill).
———, 1986. Rediscovering Tennessee: Roads Back Home and Into the Future. Introduction to the reprint of *The WPA Guide To Tennessee* (Knoxville: University of Tennessee Press).
———, 1988. Cultural Pluralism and Applied Folklore: The New Deal Precedent. In *The Conservation of Culture: Folklorists and the Private Sector*, Burt Feintuch, ed. (Lexington: University of Kentucky Press), pp. 46–67.
Hollinger, David, 1975. Ethnic Diversity, Cosmopolitanism, and the Emergence of the American Liberal Intelligentsia. *American Quarterly* 27:242–276.
Kirshenblatt-Gimblett, Barbara, 1988. Mistaken Dichotomies. *Journal of American Folklore* 101(4):140–155.

McDonald, Lois, 1928. *Southern Mill Hills: A Study of Social and Economic Forces in Certain Textile Mill Villages* (New York: A. L. Hillman).

McIllwaine, Shields, 1939. *The Southern Poor White: From Lubberland to Tobacco Road* (Norman: University of Oklahoma Press).

Murray, Chalmers S., 1937. Murray to Mabel Montgomery, July 8, 1937. Box 192, FWPNA.

Penkower, Monty, 1977. *The Federal Writers' Project: A Study in Government Patronage of the Arts* (Urbana: University of Illinois Press).

Stocking, George, 1968. *Race, Culture, and Evolution: Essays in the History of Anthropology* (New York: Free Press).

Tannenbaum, Frank, 1924. *Darker Phases of the South* (New York: G. P. Putnam's Sons).

Terrill, Tom, and Jerrold Hirsch, eds, 1978. *Such As Us: Southern Voices of the Thirties* (Chapel Hill: University of North Carolina Press).

Tindall, George B., 1967. *The Emergence of the New South, 1913–1945* (Baton Rouge: Louisiana State University Press).

History and Much, Much More: Historic and Cultural Conservation in Vicksburg, Mississippi

Ralph J. Bishop and Nancy H. Bell

Preservation of historically valuable sites and structures is but one aspect, albeit perhaps the most highly visible, of the larger issue of cultural conservation. It is also often the first to emerge in a community. In some cases, conservation may be limited to a few buildings; in others a conservation movement may develop that encompasses many areas of the community's life. In this paper we examine the development of a broad-based historic and cultural conservation movement in Vicksburg, Mississippi.

VICKSBURG'S PLACE IN HISTORY

This Mississippi River port is a site of considerable historic importance, both regionally and nationally. Founded in 1819 on a series of high loess ridges overlooking a bend in the river midway between Memphis and New Orleans, the city rapidly became a major trade and industrial center.

Vicksburg is perhaps best known as the focal point of one of the key campaigns of the American Civil War. By 1862, Confederate fortifications there had become the last major obstacle to Union control of traffic on the river; federal forces under the command of Ulysses S. Grant were charged to spare no effort in taking the town. The Vicksburg campaign culminated in a forty-seven-day siege, ending on July 4, 1863.

In addition to its military importance, the city, which grew rapidly in size in the years following the war, served as a port of entry for both goods and immigrants. Between 1860 and 1880, as much as one-third of the white population was foreign born. One in seven of Mississippi's foreign immigrants lived in Vicksburg and Warren County at this time, an area which held only four percent of the state's population.[1] The resulting diversity, which continues to the present day, is one of the things that distinguishes Vicksburg culturally from much of the rest of Mississippi.

HISTORIC PRESERVATION

Although the battlefield area surrounding the city has long been developed as a historic site (with most of it incorporated into the Vicksburg National Military Park and National Cemetery), it is only since World War II that there has been any organized concern for other aspects of Vicksburg's unique architectural and cultural heritage.

Organized support for historic preservation emerged with the formation of the Vicksburg and Warren County Historical Society in August of 1946. Its beginnings can be traced, as is so often the case, to a single citizen's actions on behalf of a threatened landmark.

In 1939, the Warren County Court House, built in 1858, was abandoned. When the county offices moved across the street to the new courthouse, serious thought was given to demolishing the old building for a parking lot. Outraged by such a possibility, a woman named Eva Whitaker Davis mounted a campaign to save the structure. On January 22, 1939, she wrote to the board of supervisors:

> I plead with you gentlemen not to make of this splendid edifice just another outmoded structure left to crumble to dust and be forgotten in the generations that march on. For cities are not remembered for their newness, but for their culture, their foresight, and their history (Cotton 1982:47).

Davis's efforts kept the issue in the public eye, and no final decision was made on the fate of the building for more than eight years.

Shortly after the Historical Society was founded, a committee of members conducted a title search of the land upon which the old courthouse sat. This search revealed that the site had been deeded to the city of Vicksburg for public use in 1825 by the Rev. John A. Lane, son-in-law and executor of the estate of Newitt Vick, the city's founder. Were the site ever to be abandoned as a public place, ownership would revert to Vick's heirs. This, along with prevailing public sentiment, persuaded the supervisors to agree to the use of the building as a museum by the Historical Society.[2] Eva Davis became the museum's first director, and the doors opened to the public on June 3, 1948 (Cotton 1982:48).

By 1958, with the museum well established, Davis and others saw a need for an organization dedicated to protecting other historic structures from demolition. Fifty people met at the museum on June 4 of that year and organized the Mississippi Historic Foundation of Vicksburg, later renamed the Vicksburg Foundation for Historic Preservation. The new foundation drew up a list of fifteen historically significant homes and asked the owners to grant it first rights to buy or seek buyers should their properties be offered for sale.

Several buildings were saved in this way during the 1960s, and by 1969 the foundation was appealing to the business community to support preservation because, as one member stated: "A five-million dollar industry [tourism] is at our disposal with very little cash outlay, and we cannot afford to let it be lost to the bulldozer."

Through the 1970s interest in preservation gained momentum. Still, several important buildings were lost, among them an 1871 synagogue. In 1973, the city passed an ordinance designating portions of downtown Vicksburg as a historic district. The ordinance was revised and strengthened in 1986 to include the establishment of a Historic Preservation Commission to oversee the designation of new districts, landmarks, and landmark sites.

The introduction of federal tax incentives for the preservation and restoration of historic buildings has helped to increase preservation activity in the 1980s. It is also possible to see a mutual enhancement between preservation and the tourist trade, which has grown threefold in volume in the last decade[3] and is now the area's second largest industry.

THE ROLE OF THE VICKSBURG FOUNDATION FOR HISTORIC PRESERVATION

In 1982 the Vicksburg Foundation for Historic Preservation hired a full-time executive director, and its activities have had a part in the establishment of several other preservation oriented agencies. Vicksburg Main Street was begun in 1984 and spearheaded by the foundation, the city, and the Chamber of Commerce. Part of a nationwide program developed by the National Trust for Historic Preservation, Main Street seeks to continue the revitalization of the historic downtown area within the context of historic preservation. The foundation was also a major force for the strengthening of the historic district ordinance and played a role in setting up the Vicksburg Board of Architectural Review to monitor rehabilitation standards and efforts.

Vicksburg Landmarks, Inc., was also established in 1984 through the foundation to provide alternatives to demolition of historic or architecturally significant structures. It sets up and maintains a revolving fund for acquisition of threatened properties and has purchased and sold to private investors three historic buildings endangered by possible demolition. It recently participated in financing the purchase and rehabilitation of three houses within a community development block grant area. Under the terms of this agreement these houses must be used for low income housing for a minimum of ten years.

BEYOND ARCHITECTURE: HISTORIC AND CULTURAL CONSERVATION

Fueled at least in part by the success of efforts to preserve historic buildings, efforts at cultural conservation have also become prominent in Vicksburg in recent years. The Historical Society and its members have been active along several fronts, particularly in the conservation of important artifacts and documents illustrating the area's history and cultural diversity. The Old Court House Museum maintains an extensive and growing archive and research library. It has recently completed an inventory of its newspaper collection as part of a statewide project directed by the Mississippi Department of Archives and History.

In 1987 the Historical Society, along with the *Vicksburg Evening Post* and the League of Women Voters, sponsored an old-fashioned political rally in Court Square, outside the museum, providing a forum for all candidates in the local primary election. The museum also serves several times a year as a venue for performances of traditional music.

Other institutional players on the preservation field include the Chamber of Commerce, the Vicksburg Convention and Visitors' Bureau, the

Council of Garden Clubs, and the public and parochial schools. "History and much, much more" is, in fact, an advertising slogan devised by the Convention and Visitors' Bureau to promote the area as a tourist and convention site. In addition to the involvement of the Chamber of Commerce, many individual businesses and business people not directly dependent on tourism, including crafts people and members of the building trades, are involved to some extent with issues of preservation and cultural conservation.

Individual and institutional interest led to the funding of two notable conservation-oriented projects in 1985 and 1986. The first of these, the Vicksburg Cultural Heritage Project, was developed by a group of local residents, many of them associated with All Saints' Episcopal School. It was funded by the National Endowment for the Humanities through the Mississippi Humanities Council. The second project, called Project Heritage, was developed by a group of teachers at the Vicksburg junior high and high schools, with funding from the International Paper Company.

The Vicksburg Cultural Heritage Project employed a cultural anthropologist full-time for nine months to explore the contributions of the city's numerous ethnic and cultural groups to its development and character and to report on his findings as widely as possible. The project resulted in a series of lectures, performances, and panel discussions; a series of leaflets on different aspects of local cultural history, several written by local experts; a biweekly newspaper column; an exhibit of photographs showing life in the area from the late nineteenth century to the present day; and a collection of videotapes.

Project Heritage sent teenagers out to interview friends, neighbors, and relatives about their lives and about traditional beliefs and practices. Two magazine-style publications resulted from this project, featuring interview reports, recipes, home remedies, and similar material. In addition, the Foundation for Historic Preservation in 1987 published a detailed and anecdote-filled walking tour guide, *Historic Vicksburg*, with the assistance of a grant-in-aid from the National Park Service.

Vicksburg High School offers a course, cosponsored by the Corps of Engineers, on the cultural and economic history of the lower Mississippi Valley. At the Vocational and Technical Center of Hinds Junior College, one of the instructors, who worked with the Vicksburg Cultural Heritage Project, has added instruction in interviewing techniques to her language arts classes. Students are asked to interview knowledgeable informants on traditional customs and then summarize their interviews in written reports.

A diversity of individual projects has also added to the conservation effort. Local historians have published several books on different aspects of the city's past (Cotton 1982; Cotton 1979; Harrell 1982; O'Neill 1976; and Philippsborn 1969). Subjects covered include the Old Court House, the U.S. Army Corps of Engineers' Waterways Experiment Station, the influence on the city of the Mississippi River, life in the early twentieth century, and the history of the area's Jewish community. Other important works in progress include a history of Vicksburg's black community by Robert Walker, the city's mayor, and a continuing series of interviews of "old-timers" by Charles Faulk, the retired managing editor of the *Vicksburg Evening Post*.

The *Post* itself is an important part of local culture and tradition, having been owned and operated by the same family since 1883. It offers extensive coverage of preservation issues and runs articles based on Faulk's interviews as a regular Sunday feature. Also appearing weekly are a column by Gordon Cotton, the director of the Old Court House Museum, and a column on genealogies of area families. Many other people not on the paper's regular staff have contributed occasional articles, and the food editor regularly publishes family recipes originating from one or another of the area's different cultural traditions.

Cemeteries have been another focus of preservation activities. In 1985 a community group began efforts to clean up, maintain, and, it is hoped, eventually restore Beulah Cemetery, the largest and possibly the oldest of the area's black burial grounds, dating back to 1863. The owner of the county's oldest funeral home has made its records, dating back to 1854, available for transcription. This task was completed in the summer of 1988 by another volunteer. A survey of area churchyards and private cemeteries is also presently being undertaken.

A number of area churches, some of which occupy architecturally notable buildings, have issued publications recounting their histories. A major contribution in this area has been a compilation of histories of Warren County's black churches put together by Rev. H. B. Dotson, Sr.

WHY PRESERVE?

Preservation and conservation in Vicksburg can be viewed from two basic perspectives. The first is the importance of heritage and how people view their past. The second is economics: preservation has turned out to be good for business.

The story of Eva Davis and the Old Court House exemplifies the first approach, and many people become involved in preservation through a love of architecture that is aesthetically pleasing and a sense that certain buildings literally define home. Similarly, people may see in cultural conservation links to a homeland receding in personal or ancestral memory, or links to a time now vanished and a way of life unalterably changing. It is this connection between conservation and a sense of personal or community identity which stimulates the thousands of hours of individual, volunteer research and participation in community projects of the sort mentioned above.

As noted before, there is considerable business activity in Vicksburg, particularly in the tourist industry, that ties directly into preservation. Antebellum homes, carefully restored with period furnishings, serve as inns, bed and breakfast houses, and architectural showpieces. City planners see preservation putting properties back on the tax rolls; bankers and property owners see rehabilitation, properly done, as a good investment. Such people often offer more than lip service to the cause of preservation. Local officials and business people serve actively on the boards of the Historical Society and the Foundation for Historic Preservation.

In the fall of 1988, it was announced that a multimillion-dollar development, Southern Heritage Trust, featuring an 1850s theme park, is being planned for a site near Vicksburg. Such a project would be unlikely to become a reality in a community obsessed solely with the past, or looking only toward the future. How great an influence the preservationists will have upon the shape it ultimately takes, time will tell.

Always, though, there is conflict. A local preservationist walks a very thin tightrope, balancing between his or her responsibility to preserve as much of the built environment as possible and the need to be flexible and not appear to be an unreasonable "hysterical preservationist." Compromise is necessary, but the basic responsibility is to save what is valuable and cannot be replaced. One must be progressive and bend in areas where the resource is marginally important in order to save "lying down in front of the bulldozer" for that which is essential. One of the apparent reasons for the influence of the preservation movement in Vicksburg is that from the outset, local preservationists have had a fine sense of when to "lie down in front of the bulldozer."

NOTES

1. This statement is based on several sources, particularly the records of the 1860, 1870, and 1880 censuses. Also see Smith 1968.
2. The Vick estate was a genuine can of worms. Newitt Vick had thirteen children, and they battled over his will for decades.
3. As reported by the Convention and Visitors' Bureau, based on receipts from a one percent county hotel and restaurant tax.

REFERENCES

Cotton, Gordon, 1982. *The Old Court House* (Raymond, Miss.: Keith Printing Co.).
Cotton, Jane, 1979. *A History of the Waterways Experiment Station* (Vicksburg: U.S. Army Corps of Engineers Waterways Experiment Station).
Dotson, H. B., Sr., 1983. History of Churches (Unpublished ms. available at Old Court House Museum, Vicksburg).
Harrell, Virginia Calohan, 1982. *Vicksburg and the River* (Jackson: University Press of Mississippi).
O'Neill, J. Cyril, 1976. *Early Twentieth Century Vicksburg, 1900–1910* (Raymond, Miss.: Keith Printing Co.).
Philippsborn, Gertrude, 1969. *History of the Jewish Community in Vicksburg* (Vicksburg: by the author).
Smith, Claude P., 1968. Immigration into Mississippi During Reconstruction (M.A. thesis, Mississippi College, Clinton).

Writing Popular History: Contrasting Approaches from Rural Mississippi and Rural Canada

Seena B. Kohl

This paper compares the Mississippi Committee for the Humanities Scholar-in-Residence Project in Neshoba County, Mississippi, with Canadian local history projects conducted in rural Saskatchewan and Alberta.[1] In both settings, there was an underlying shared assumption that knowledge about the past and recognition of persons commonly overlooked in the writing of history stimulate historic consciousness and pride in one's community. In both settings, individual experience within the family or community reinforced generational ties.

Both regions, the semi-arid cattle and wheat region of southeastern Alberta and southwestern Saskatchewan and the small farm, clay hill region of Neshoba County in central Mississippi, are areas with histories of intense economic and social struggles. In both settings people remained spatially if not socially isolated until the mid-1950s. Both experienced economic hardship, migration of people out of the locality, an aging population, lack of opportunities for young people, and disappearing small villages, all common rural experiences. Both locales have been subject to social disparagement from more affluent parts of their respective nations. Migrants from this Canadian region during the 1930s depression had the same national status as "Okies" in the United States,[2] while the civil rights movement placed Neshoba County on the map as the epitome of white brutality.

Today Neshoba County is composed of 71 percent white, 20 percent black and 9 percent Choctaw Indian. It remains the center of the Mississippi Band of Choctaw, the descendants of those Choctaw who refused to be removed west of the Mississippi despite the 1830 Treaty of Dancing Rabbit Creek. Few of those who remained were able to secure land, however, and they maintained a marginal subsistence in isolated areas of the county until awarded tribal status under the Indian Reorganization Act of 1934 (Kohl 1986a; Peterson 1971). The white population descends from small farmers; the black population consists largely of descendants of the slaves who accompanied early white settlers and freed blacks who entered the county after slavery as small landholders and sharecroppers. Despite gradual industrialization in the past two decades, Neshoba County shares problems common to most rural areas —an aging population and lack of local opportunities for all its young people.

Neshoba County became nationally known as "Bloody Neshoba" when three civil rights workers were murdered there in 1964. White (and some black) county residents share with other Southerners a defensive posture regarding the view "outsiders" have of them. They also share with other Southerners (black and white) a sense of pride and a continued stake in their local community and state.

In the Mississippi humanities program, at the initiative of the local community, a scholar from the humanities is placed in a rural community for an extended period of time. The goal of the Neshoba County project, "Diverse Origins, Common History," was to develop appreciation and understanding among the White, Afro-American, and Mississippi Choctaw populations. Recognizing their shared history of segregation and violence, the project was directed toward enabling county residents to look back as well as move forward together.

In the Saskatchewan and Alberta projects, local volunteer committees produced community history books celebrating homestead settlement. Most books were part of the provincial celebrations and were sponsored by programs concerned with historical resources and the New Horizons Program of Health and Welfare Canada directed toward senior citizens' groups. The aim of the latter was to "encourage retired Canadians to become more actively involved in the life of their community" (Health and Welfare Canada 1978:2). Small grants from the New Horizons Program were available, but the funds for research, publicity, and publication costs were raised locally.

The present-day residents of southeastern Alberta and southwestern Saskatchewan are, for the most part, descendents of the original homestead population. This area of the Canadian plains was the last large portion of North America to be permanently settled, with cattlemen arriving in the 1880s and the great majority of homesteaders arriving between 1909 and 1912. As with Great Plains settlement elsewhere in the United States and Canada, the initial optimism produced by cheap land was belied by the limited agricultural potential of the initial small, 160-acre homestead tracts. The variability and uncertainty of climate, particularly rainfall, created special hazards for agriculture with intermittent droughts. Widespread abandonment of land occurred before a reasonable degree of social and economic stability was obtained (Bicha 1968; Fowke 1947; Macintosh 1934). The struggles of residents' ancestors to establish family agricultural enterprises remain vivid and are exemplified in family stories. The provincial local history and heritage projects and the local community history books build upon this interest.

THE CANADIAN PRODUCT: COMMUNITY SPONSORED LOCAL HISTORY BOOKS

In Canada, provincial and federal encouragement to record community history resulted in committee-organized, collectively written, and locally produced history books. These books are compendiums of family history and community events and range in size from short pamphlets to five to six hundred page hard-bound volumes. By 1983 there were more than eight hundred books for the province of Alberta alone (Krotki 1983). The Regina, Saskatchewan, public library's Prairie History Room has compiled a bibliographic and location aid to local and district histories that lists more than seven hundred volumes.

For the most part, the editors, overwhelmingly women, are without previous research, writing, editing, or publishing experience. They do, however, have a plethora of organizational skills, honed in previous work in community volunteer associations, as well as commitment to their local community. They are the "stayers" and their descendants. While they recognize hardships, they are more interested in celebrating survival in the face of hardships, emphasizing success, and ignoring, to the degree possible, the failures. There is shared agreement that the settlement of their part of the country "made history" and should not be forgotten. For example, the dedication page of one community history reads: "In deciding to prepare this book, the committee determined that the history of this corner would not be forgotten; that the people, their labours, their perseverance and their achievements should not go unrecognized and unremembered" (Lanz and Kusler 1982:iii). The idea of "making history" is not only a retrospective view, but is present in letters and diaries of homesteaders.

Organization of community history projects was similar in virtually all localities. Announcements of organizational meetings were placed in the local newspaper by the initiating club or by interested individuals. School districts formed at the time of homestead settlement commonly were used as the basis for the formation of committees, each school district selecting a representative who then became responsible for contacting the families in that district. Where the initial homesteader or family was not found, the usual practice was to have some old-timer write a short comment about the individual or the family. In some cases the homestead papers were used to determine ethnic origins and proper names. Inevitably some persons were missed, but the larger volumes have an impressive completeness.

The degree to which complete representation was achieved depended on locating key family members willing to take responsibility for writing their family history (and the ability of these key people to elicit cooperation from their kin group). The all inclusiveness of the histories also depended on whether or not the writers perceived as part of the community those living outside the formal community associational life of church, school, or political organization (Indians, Chinese, Jews, Metis, and other minority ethnic groups). In general the histories do not include such groups except to note their unique characteristics which placed these residents outside the community structure (Kohl 1986b; Oliver et al. 1984).

THE MISSISSIPPI PRODUCT: LIBRARY RESOURCES AND A VISUAL EXHIBIT

The Mississippi project involved interaction between the scholar and local residents, each learning from the other (Mitchell and Hiatt 1984). A sixteen-member steering committee composed of representatives from the initiating groups and other community members met monthly with the scholar to review activities and set priorities. Rather than writing and publishing a community history book, key goals were stimulation of interest in and development of historical resources for the three resident population groups and preparation of a visual display of the county's history and heritage. Committee members provided introductions and identified local resources and community support for the scholar; nevertheless, the primary tasks of publicizing the project and its goals, organizing, and collecting data were left to the scholar, as were public presentation of the local historical experience through talks, newspaper columns, and the exhibit.

County residents were involved in the collection of family, school and church documents, and photographs. Letters, diaries, reminiscences, poll tax receipts and other legal notices, photographs, and family genealogies were brought to the project office in the county library, copied, and placed on file in the library for shared use. Also on file are interviews with individuals who experienced particular events such as school desegregation and sharecropping and with persons knowledgeable about specific topics such as midwifery, rolling stores, folk medicine, or Choctaw material culture.

The exhibit is a twelve-panel photographic montage, using for the most part pictures received from descendants of the non-slave owning white families who operated small farms. They were family portraits, taken for the most part between 1903 and 1920, before the age of the snapshot, by photographers who peddled their services throughout the county. There were few pictures of Choctaw and black families, indications of their relative economic status. Those gaps were filled in with pictures from the Farm Security Administration taken during the 1930s, from the Tuskeegee Institute Archives, from the Smithsonian Archives, and from the Mississippi State Archives.

The photo montage attracted considerable attention; more than twenty thousand persons viewed it at the Choctaw and Neshoba County fairs. A common sight was grandparents from all population groups pointing out to their grandchildren the type of house they lived in, the type of school they attended, and the way work was done when they were children. Because no names were associated with the pictures (a decision of the scholar initially questioned by committee members and others), all populations could identify similar aspects of their lives.

THE PROJECTS COMPARED

Both projects encouraged the individuals who lived the experiences to interpret, record, and position their past lives in some form of historical record. Both were based upon the knowledge of expertise held within the community. Both emphasized the importance of ordinary people in building and maintaining communities, and both encouraged recognition and appreciation of the valiant efforts of previous generations.

While the Canadian project emphasized the experience of settlement and establishment of communities by family groups as an important aspect of history, the Neshoba County project, through involving local residents and recognizing their families' participation in county history, de-emphasized the traditional institutional history of elites. A dominant theme in the scholar's talks and newspaper columns was to have people rethink history and their relationship to it, rethink the ways in which Neshoba County was both unique and similar to other places, and relate personal events to events in the wider social world.

Material for the weekly newspaper column was selected from the interviews to illustrate how events in the past affected different populations or community development. The columns began with specific experience and then moved toward generalizations: the personal experience of road building and its connection with social change, the experience of being the first black woman hired at the local factory and its connection with later economic development and desegregation, or quotes from a set of love letters used to discuss changes in gender and generational roles.

In the Canadian communities, the product is clearly one of local and volunteer creation, and as such has generated great pride. Critics express concern with the antiquarian character of the books, with nostalgic reminiscences passing for clarity of cause and effect, with the ignoring of unpleasant, "embarrassing," or controversial aspects of a population's experience (Bowsfield 1969; Oliver et al. 1984; Voisey 1985). While these critical comments are meaningful from the point of view of the historian, they are irrelevant from the point of view of the participants. The occasion of publishing such a volume was used by the members of rural communities as a way of witnessing their collective experience rather than producing an academic history. And family experiences were the base for that collective experience, in part as a consequence of family homesteaders having settled the region.

The community local history book projects did not originally anticipate the production of *family* histories. In fact, as Stiles (1985:13) notes, "the prominence given to individual and family stories . . . runs counter to the recommendations" given in both workshops and materials available from the Alberta Historical Resources Division. Project organizers assumed that the product would be community histories in which the goal would be to "record the origin, growth and perhaps decline of a community . . . to identify the factors that have given your community its character and identity" (*Exploring Local History in Saskatchewan* 1985:1). Despite guidelines encouraging a thematic or subject approach, however, the editors who were surveyed remained unabashed about the emphasis devoted to family sagas and genealogy, because their intent was to be able to "follow families."

Community history books are read by locals to settle family arguments and to understand and transmit to others the connections between local populations. They are used by ministers and funeral directors to sort out family connections and by families in the same way family photograph albums are used. Just as family albums do not picture the conflicts and controversies (except indirectly), neither do these history albums. For the most part, they present a collective recollection of a past in which community and altruism played a larger part than they do today. Invariably, they imply or state explicitly that although the past was hard, it was positive. Many claim that those were the best years of their lives. More than mere nostalgia, this elevation of the past serves as the vehicle for criticism of present mores (Oliver et al. 1984).

These local histories represent a distinctive type of literature. They attempt to recapture the homestead period (a facet of the relatively recent past of western settlement and one that is idealized in national myths) with its creation of opportunities for all. Settlement history seeks to fulfill an egalitarian imperative by including all those who shared the homestead experience, even those who left the region. Despite experiences of hostility and tension among immigrants who were linguistically, culturally, and religiously different from the Anglo-Saxon Protestant majority on the Canadian frontier (Palmer 1982), the local community histories ignore this aspect and create a past with little discord or difference.

Nevertheless, all are not included. Prior to European colonization, this region provided a homeland for Native American hunting populations: Cree, Nez Perce, Gros Ventre, and Assiniboine among others. There are many reminders of these earlier peoples in place names, reserves set aside, and special social and welfare programs; however, despite their visible presence, as a group they are ignored and unrecognized as part of the local communities (Braroe 1975).

In interviews, book editors reported explicit agreements among the committee members to avoid differences or controversy. The editors were warned about libel by their local printer or publisher's agent and attempted to steer a middle course between "making things interesting" and "staying out of trouble." With rare exceptions, the past was endowed with a *post hoc* harmony. Where individuals in conflict with (or outside) the larger group are not omitted from community history books, they are transformed symbolically into "local characters," cleaned up and repackaged as special, unique, or even mythical. This repackaging glosses over past schisms and past conflicts, permitting the community to be presented as a harmonious whole (Kohl 1986b).

In contrast, local history in the South, in which slavery, inequality, and oppression of the poor and non-white played so important a role, cannot offer the possibility of similar collective representations of an egalitarian past. Yet there were some similarities in the perception of the past. Many in each group felt that *within their own ethnic group,* people cared more for each other and less for things, shared more, were kinder and somehow "better" people in the past. In general (for the white population) "things were less complicated." In this context, the role of the scholar as outsider became one of "cultural broker," communicating the experiences of one population to another.

Participants gained an increased understanding of the lives of others and the economic and social struggles of the past. For some, this meant a new appreciation for the struggles of parent sharecroppers and a change from embarrassment about family poverty to a sense of pride in achievement. For others, it amounted to a new appreciation of the Choctaw experience, or recognition of the valor of participants in the early struggles for desegregation.

There is no doubt that given the heritage of differential power relations between white and black and Choctaw and the segregation of the three groups, a history of Neshoba County including all three populations could not have been depicted without outside assistance. The focus on families in the Neshoba project was a consequence of the explicit goal of including all groups and avoiding the trap of emphasizing white, elite community leaders. When history is not considered to be the product of elites, the daily lives of ordinary people, prominently including women, become the center of attention. Home and family enterprises (in Neshoba County the small-scale, marginal farm) became the unit of study. Using this approach, changes in societal norms can be viewed through the lens of their impact on daily life.

While the Neshoba project had no specific product to "hand down," send to family in other states, or leave on the coffee table, the resources for examining county history remain one of the more tangible aspects of the project. These resources, located in the county library, include previously published and unpublished data: Master's theses, Ph.D. dissertations, research reports, traveler's accounts, autobiographies, and essays. Of course, availability of material does not ensure its future use.

CONCLUSION: THE CONCEPT OF "HISTORY" AND ITS MEANING FOR COMMUNITY

While the Canadian and Mississippi programs value community participation in recording and examining their heritage, the organizational procedures differed as did the final products. These differences reflect an inherent tension between an external macrosocial perspective and that of the local participants.

In the Canadian projects, despite the programmatic goals of provincial heritage councils, local responses were to create their own version of history. "History" in the Canadian projects became identified as personal and family experience. The absence of an outside perspective narrowed the community's vision about historical process. Although all the books include some material about the chronological development of community, the local writers were more interested in preserving the record of real identified people than in painting a wider picture. In part this emphasis may be a consequence of the rural character of the books. While the editors, writers, and organizers perceived the decline and disappearance of towns and institutions (this being one stimulus for writing the books), they were not interested in macrosocial or economic forces to explain or document the process. At the same time, involvement in writing the books was a learning process. Editors reported that they changed their views of history after finishing the product, and became more critical about what could or should have been done.

In Mississippi, the presence of an outside expert, while ensuring connections between the experience of the individuals and the context of external or social structural features, meant less local responsibility and less ownership of the collected materials. Although Neshoba County residents were encouraged to write their reminiscences of events, there was little of the same level of participation as in the Canadian projects. The primary responsibility remained the scholar's.

Nevertheless, in both programs, there was a shared appreciation and recognition of the economic and social struggles of previous generations. In the Canadian setting an unanticipated, but important, consequence spurred by the publication of the books was the re-establishment of past ties through letters, phone calls, and visits of old friends and neighbors, community festivals and reunions. Above all, the books are seen as a tangible invocation to children not to forget the past efforts of their families.

In the Mississippi case, family ties have, despite considerable urban migration, remained strong among all three populations. The maintenance and importance of these ties, in fact, characterize Southern rural life. Yet the content of these ties did change with the public presentation of past racial conflict and economic stress, matters not commonly nor comfortably discussed among families or close friends. In addition, the conceptual value of a de-institutionalized history was introduced, and the resources for such history remain accessible. In its most positive and optimistic sense, popular history in both settings, "gives history back to the people in their own words. And in giving a past, it also helps them towards a future of their own making" (Thompson 1978:226).

NOTES

1. The research for the Canadian part of this paper was funded by the National Endowment for the Humanities as part of a three-year project titled "The Northern Plains Culture History Project." Surveys from thirty-six Canadian community book editors and ten interviews were collected between 1985

and 1987. The data for the Mississippi part of the paper were collected during 1981 while I served as Scholar-in-Residence for Neshoba County. Courtney Tannehill, head librarian for the Neshoba County Public Library, members of the Brown Bag Reading Group, and the Neshoba County Historical Society, with the aid of John Peterson from Mississippi State University, developed the proposal for the project.

2. The area has been termed an "economic and social deficit" region (Kraenzel 1967). As of 1931, compared to other Canadian provinces (excluding Newfoundland), Saskatchewan and Alberta had the lowest level of living in terms of electricity, piped-in water supply, mechanical refrigerators, and flush toilets (Royal Commission on Agriculture and Rural Life 1956:31). The population remained (as in similar "deficit areas") independent and stubborn. With few exceptions, they did not perceive of themselves as living in a poverty pocket, although they almost universally acknowledged that they had neither money nor resources. They coped with a shortage of resources, help, and attention until the recent past, when the general prosperity of both Canada and the United States began to benefit the neglected agrarian northwest.

REFERENCES

Bicha, Karel D., 1968. *The American Farmer and the Canadian West* (Lawrence, Kans.: Coronado Press).

Bowsfield, Hartwell, 1969. Writing Local History. *Alberta Historical Review* 17: 10–19.

Braroe, Neils, 1975. *Indian and White: Self Image and Interaction in a Canadian Plains Community* (Palo Alto, Calif.: Stanford University Press).

Exploring Local History in Saskatchewan, 2d ed., 1985. (Regina and Saskatoon: Saskatchewan Archives Board).

Fowke, Vernon C., 1947. *An Introduction to Canadian Agricultural History* (Toronto: University of Toronto Press).

Health and Welfare Canada, 1978. *New Horizons*. Pamphlet Cat. N. H77–3/1978 (Ottawa: Minister of Supply and Services Canada).

Kohl, Seena B., 1986a. Ethnocide and Ethnogenesis: A Case Study of the Mississippi Band of Choctaw, a Genocide Avoided. *Holocaust and Genocide Studies* 1:91–100.

———, 1986b. Writing Local History: the Creation of a Shared Past. Paper presented at the *Palliser Triangle Conference*, Medicine Hat College, Medicine Hat, Alberta, Canada.

Kraenzel, Carl F., 1967. Deficit-creating Influences for Role Performance and

Status Acquisition in Sparsely Populated Regions of the United States. In *Symposium on the Great Plains of North America*, C. C. Zimmerman and S. Russell, eds. (Fargo: North Dakota State University), pp. 168–179.

Krotki, Joanna E., 1983. *An Annotated Bibliography of Local Histories in Alberta*, 2d ed. (Calgary: University of Alberta, Department of Slavic and East European Studies).

Lanz, Olive and Beatrice Kusler, eds., 1982. *The Forgotten Corner: A History of the Communities of Comrey, Catchem, Hooper-Pendland, Onefour, Wild Horse (also including the Range Land), Townships One to Four, Ranges One to Six* (Medicine Hat, Alb.: The New Horizons Committee).

Mackintosh, W. A., 1934. *Prairie Settlement: The Geographic Background*. vol. 1, *Canadian Frontiers of Settlement* (Toronto: Macmillan).

Mitchell, Dennis and Jane Crater Hiatt, 1984. *Mississippi Scholar-In-Residence Projects History and Handbook* (Jackson, Miss.: Mississippi Committee for the Humanities).

Oliver, Barbara, Mark Vigrass, Wendy Whelan, and Michele Young, 1984. *Regional Heritage Project: A Content Analysis of Selected Local Histories in Saskatchewan* (Regina, Sask.: Canadian Plains Research Center, University of Regina).

Palmer, Howard, 1982. *Patterns of Prejudice: A History of Nativism in Alberta* (Toronto: McClelland and Stewart).

Peterson, John H. Jr., 1971. The Indian in the Old South. In *Red, White and Black: Symposium on Indians in the Old South,* Charles M. Hudson, ed. (Athens: University of Georgia Press), pp. 116–133.

Royal Commission on Agriculture and Rural Life, 1956. *The Home and Family in Rural Saskatchewan,* Report no. 10, Government of Saskatchewan (Regina: Queen's Printer).

Stiles, Joanne A., 1985. *Gilded Memories: Perceptions of the Frontier in Rural Alberta as Reflected in Popular History* (M.A. thesis, University of Alberta, Edmonton).

Thompson, Paul, 1978. *The Voice of the Past: Oral History* (Oxford: Oxford University Press).

Voisey, Paul, 1985. Rural Local History and the Prairie West. *Prairie Forum* 10:327–338.

New Ways for Old: Assessing Contributions of the Tennessee Community Heritage Project

Betty J. Duggan

The Tennessee Humanities Council (THC) encouraged the examination of America's past within a broad interdisciplinary framework in its award-winning program, the Tennessee Community Heritage Project (TCHP).[1] Through this project between 1983 and 1986, interested communities, organizations, and individuals throughout Tennessee received free, full-time assistance in researching and interpreting selected aspects of their heritage.

Large-scale, academically supervised public history projects are not without precedent in America (Brumberg 1982; Hart 1978; Sand 1978), but the TCHP took community heritage programming into uncharted territory in its range of professional services, participants, interpretive media, and interdisciplinary approach. The underlying premise of the TCHP was assisting Tennessee's adults to identify, examine, record, and interpret untapped cultural and historical resources in new and interesting ways. Such an objective was purposely subject to many interpretations. Each community's desires, real information gaps, and volunteer group composition and experience determined the direction and intensity of assistance provided by the TCHP staff. This "from the bottom up" approach allowed the staff to help reshape and expand ideas which originated at the local level. Through forging a partnership with the public it sought to serve, the TCHP was able in a brief time to involve thousands of Tennesseans as active participants in preparing local history exhibits, books, lecture series, conferences, workshops, festivals, radio series, and photographic copying days; as many as one million more people were reached as audience members of these activities, projects, and events.

The mainstay of the TCHP organization was its regional Scholar-in-Residence program. While the TCHP was coordinated through a special position at the THC's Nashville office, each scholar's daily operations were carried out through a grant to a local college or university. The TCHP team originally included five historians, one anthropologist, a folklorist, and a specialist in preservation education. After the first year, however, the composition of the staff changed dramatically, in large part due to the fieldwork orientation of the job, with three social historians, three anthropologists, and one folklorist completing the project. All had to learn how to work with clients by varying their approach. For instance, on an especially busy day a scholar might meet in the morning to review the progress and problems of a church group collecting oral histories, give a lunch-time publicity talk to a civic club, and that evening conduct a workshop in "reading" historic photographs, all in different communities. Such constant interaction with the lay public in a multiplicity of settings was particularly difficult for those scholars who had worked only in a classroom setting or in carrying out personal research. In this respect, especially at the beginning, the anthropologists and folklorists with their extensive fieldwork experience were at an advantage. However, through informal communications, staff reports and meetings, enrichment sessions, and occasional joint community or regional projects, the TCHP scholars were soon sharing special expertise and experiences. While it is true that the scholars worked as a team in many ways, because of local circumstances each scholar really had to create and manage a miniature TCHP, taking account of the distinct geographical features, settlement histories, economic foci, social agendas, and historical interests found within each of the state's three geo-political divisions of east, middle, and west Tennessee.

PROGRAMMING AS PARTNERSHIP

Establishing an identity for the TCHP through the news media, building a network of community contacts, and developing client rapport occupied much of the first half-year. Assistance as initially conceived

—teaching new views of what history is, how to formulate relevant questions about the past, stressing the importance and relationship of "nearby" history to larger issues—had to be the last step in the scholars' work, not the first. Indeed, the idea of assistance had to be thought of in much broader terms, for even groups eager to take advantage of the TCHP's services often had great difficulty in selecting a topic, formulating questions, and undertaking research. One scholar reported, "It gradually dawned on me that I would have to lower my expectations considerably as to what these groups were capable of doing." My own experiences suggested to me that, in all but the most extreme cases, "changed tactics," rather than "lowered expectations," was more apropos to the situation. Finding compromises that did not eliminate or trivialize a project's academic value but which still met with community approval and enthusiasm continually challenged our creativity, and sometimes our patience.

Most scholars spent a great deal of time trying to interest groups not traditionally included as participants in or subjects of status quo local history studies. One scholar was especially interested in involving urban ethnics, senior citizens, and the handicapped. Others showed a personal interest in community projects focusing on women's history, religious history, or the expansion of program emphases in existing historical societies. My own special commitments were encouraging small towns, rural or mountain communities, and involving blacks, Indians, and working-class whites to develop projects. Through these special efforts and intense publicity campaigns an ever-increasing number and kind of organizations (historical societies, museums, arts councils, churches, schools, libraries, senior citizens centers, public radio stations, colleges and universities, performing arts groups, and even one mental health organization) sought TCHP assistance. The programs and services eventually developed to meet the needs of these varied clients basically fell into four categories: public talks and lecture series, workshops and conferences, consultations and technical services, and project development and implementation. In discussing these categories, I draw on personal experiences in a few of the approximately one hundred communities and neighborhoods in southeastern Tennessee with which I worked.

The TCHP scholars were invited to speak to a variety of organizations, a task most of us found enjoyable and worthwhile. One scholar reported, "One aspect of this work that I have especially begun to like is my role as the person who in endlessly different ways talks to diverse groups about, 'What is history? How do you study it? How do you ask a good question? What are some questions that might be asked?' This, I now think, is one of our most valuable challenges. Our audiences are diverse and, thus, one is never certain what form will best communicate the message."

Historical societies and educators, in particular, requested that the TCHP scholars present formal lectures which focused on topics such as Tennessee's prehistoric inhabitants, women's history, or the history of Southern Jews. TCHP scholars were also instrumental in organizing guest lecture series such as a day-long program on the agricultural and industrial history of Dyer County in west Tennessee or the establishment of a speakers' bureau in the Upper Cumberland region of middle Tennessee. Expanding on the lecture format, in conjunction with the University of Tennessee at Chattanooga's public radio station, a local radio announcer and I co-hosted a thirteen part series featuring some of the state's foremost scholars discussing the prehistoric, geographical, historical, political, religious, economic, artistic, musical, linguistic, and ethnic heritage of Tennesseans.

Lecture series were also used as a complement to other types of programming as in the case of a THC grant awarded to the Etowah Arts Commission. Originally, this group wanted funding to rent an Appalshop photographic exhibit, "Appalachian Women: Three Generations." In order to balance the cultural perspective projected in these prepared posters from the Central Appalachian area, I assisted the local group in developing a temporary exhibition which dealt with twentieth-century women in the home, workplace, religion, fine arts, and folk arts in their own Southern Appalachian valley town. Accompanying the exhibits were public lectures on Appalachian women in fiction by a prominent regional author, a historical and ethnographic overview of the region's women by a historian, and a discussion on Appalachian women in labor struggles led by a sociologist. The popularity of these activities later spurred this arts organization to co-sponsor TCHP photographic copying days and research workshops for their whole county, and more recently to pursue a second grant for a permanent exhibit about their own town (population 3,758) which was created eighty-five years ago as a regional headquarters by the Louisville and Nashville Railroad.

Among the most effective and popular means the TCHP used for conveying how to do quality research were the two-hour workshop and the one-day training conference. Workshops focusing on oral history, written documents, historical photographs, family history, folklore, and material culture were developed first. Later sessions dealt with more specialized topics—church histories, cemetery studies, local history museums, and preparing exhibits and audiovisual presentations. Most workshops took place in locations where even poorly educated community members felt comfortable—community centers, churches, local schools, and libraries. Although workshops usually were given at the request of a particular organization, several scholars tried to develop and promote a logical sequence for their various workshops, as in the case of a continuing education course on local history research offered in northwest Tennessee.

The Scholars-in-Residence also found that presenting one workshop in a community could lead to the development of a full-scale project. Such was the case of Ducktown, a remote community of 583 persons. During the first months of the TCHP, I conducted a workshop for the Ducktown Basin Museum attended by three people. Nearly two years later the same organization turned to the TCHP again, this time for assistance in reinterpreting some of their displays. The result was an exhibit and lecture series funded by the THC that spanned the changing lifestyles and fortunes of local Indians from prehistoric times through the early twentieth century. "Native Americans of the Copper Basin" opened in time to be part of the joint Miner's Homecoming–Homecoming '86 activities for three Basin communities. To date over six thousand visitors from the United States and several foreign countries have seen the exhibit, but the project's impact does not end in statistics. With this grant serving as a benchmark for the kind of programming this volunteer organization had always wanted, its board lobbied for state support. In March 1988 the Ducktown Basin Museum officially became a state-owned facility which will soon operate under a local board and full-time director.

Because of the demand for the "doing history" workshops, one-day conferences were developed to serve larger multi-county audiences. Prominent lay historians, regional authors, or well-established humanities professionals were often used as drawing cards for these highly popular events. An illustration of this approach is the East Tennessee

Community Heritage Conference held at Cleveland State Community College which I developed a few months into the TCHP project. John Edgerton, author of a popular, nonfiction work about one Kentucky family's history, was brought in to address several hundred people at three engagements in Chattanooga and Cleveland. The next day he joined staff members of the East Tennessee Historical Society and five TCHP scholars in conducting lectures, workshops, and discussion sessions for approximately ninety participants from thirty different communities. Among those attending were housewives, retired persons, schoolteachers, civic leaders, and local government officials. Media coverage and good conference attendance for this event, which occurred during the early months of the TCHP, gave the project legitimacy in the regional public's eye and subsequent entrance into several new communities.

It was not unusual for the scholars to meet with individuals or groups only once or twice. In such brief consultations we always tried to leave these people with concrete suggestions, technical materials, or professional contacts to help them, whether their concern was preserving county documents or historic structures. Several TCHP scholars also helped found county historical societies where none existed. In these situations the scholars usually provided advice on society formation, as well as helped to secure the first few speakers. Throughout the TCHP's existence, photographic copying services were also offered to groups starting historic photograph collections, doing exhibits, or needing to illustrate a local history book. Communities were asked only to supply and develop the film and provide local volunteers to record information about each photograph's content, context, and ownership. Often a workshop on reading historic photographs was scheduled to coincide with these sessions, or hand-outs on the preservation and interpretation of photographs were distributed.

Technical and interpretive resource materials were distributed by the TCHP at workshops, conferences, and on request. While there was a lot of interchange and re-working of materials among the scholars, all developed their own special packets to suit clients' needs. For example, at the beginning of the project I prepared a "doing community history" packet which was sent out to all of the Homecoming '86 heritage groups in my region; another scholar designed audiovisual and written materials for the state's social science and humanities teachers; and several

TCHP scholars prepared historical bibliographies for the counties in their area.

PROJECT DEVELOPMENT AND IMPLEMENTATION

A great deal of controversy existed among our scholars concerning lay groups applying for grants: Could a group treat its chosen topic in a significant manner? What previous research experience did its members have? Was there local commitment of time, money, or deadline flexibility? Often the scholars felt more comfortable encouraging communities to develop projects which were limited in research and financial scope and funded locally. Where TCHP scholars thought groups were ready to undertake in-depth studies, grant funds were sought. Projects receiving THC funding included a range of topics and approaches: for example, a folklife festival featuring local musicians, crafts demonstrations, an interpretive booklet, and displays in northwest Tennessee's Reelfoot Lake area which drew a weekend crowd of ten thousand people; an exhibit on black education in the middle Tennessee hometown of the KKK; a slide-tape program on the contributions of women leaders in a mountain county; and an exhibit and lecture series on changing recreation and leisure-time patterns in another small town. Two grant projects which I worked with illustrate TCHP program development assistance and some of the associated problems.

Members of the Sweetwater Homecoming '86 Heritage Committee, most of whom were retired business people or housewives, were asked by their city administrators to establish a museum using the city's Homecoming '86 theme—"Transportation Come Alive." Totally baffled by this theme and not knowing how to begin a museum, the committee turned to the TCHP. Initial discussions revealed that transportation was a logical starting point, since from Sweetwater's founding as a pre-Civil War railroad town every aspect of its community life had been touched by transportation changes through the years. Instead of jumping straight into a museum project, however, I persuaded the committee to explore local interests, capabilities, and resources by first developing a permanent exhibit.

After extensive discussion and editing sessions with the chairpersons, a successful THC grant application was completed. Few of the volunteers had conducted local history research, and those who had were not necessarily schooled in examining the nature of everyday history or how community interaction could be seen in the historic written and material record. Grant funds helped to remedy this by providing another anthropologist, two historians, and an exhibit designer to assist me in training and reviewing the volunteers' documentary, oral history, artifactual, and photographic storyline research. The strongest components of the volunteers' research were the oral histories they collected, a task which they enjoyed and felt comfortable in doing, and the photographic copying days which they organized. Volunteers were least at ease in the difficult tasks of data analysis and exhibit text composition. With opening day rapidly approaching I intervened, reviewed the materials, and took the lead in writing the exhibit text with the two chairpersons critiquing and editing me instead of the other way around as had been planned. In contrast, the chairpersons, community volunteers, and city officials played the major role in acquiring and renovating the exhibition hall and fabricating the exhibit.

The result of this effort was a visually pleasing and informative exhibit relating changing transportation modes to the town's founding, occupational opportunities, economics, agriculture, social life, entertainment, and government services. One of the most satisfying moments personally in this two-year project came when more than five hundred people from this town of 4,725, ranging from the mayor to auto mechanics and from young middle-class whites to elderly blacks, attended the exhibit opening. Subsequently, during the city's Homecoming '86 activities eight to ten thousand people from twenty-eight states and two foreign countries saw the exhibit. Since that time the accompanying interpretive brochure and bibliography have been used in the local school system's Tennessee history course; the county historical society and home demonstration club have had special programs centered on the exhibit; and temporary displays of Depression-era toys, whittling, and historical firearms have been shown on site. Today a newly established museum board is preparing with city funding to open a second permanent exhibit following the model of research and design they learned through their TCHP-assisted project.

Another project, called "Clinton: An Identity Rediscovered," provides an example of TCHP work with a group interested in writing about local history. This Homecoming '86 Heritage Committee from a town of 5,345 persons was composed primarily of educators. Drawing on this expertise, we fashioned a successful THC proposal to publish a collection of essays on various themes related to Clinton's historical growth and change. From the initial training sessions, through the numerous chapter outlines, drafts, and the final essays, three professional historians and I worked with each research team to challenge them to think in new ways about old interests. In particular we stressed history as an ongoing process, the community as part of a larger world, and the need to deal with the ugly events in a community's past as well as with its more glorious moments. This counseling paid off in a product which examined not only important dates, names, and public figures in the community's past, but the local impact of national trends and events such as the Civil War, prohibition, the technological and educational changes introduced when the neighboring Oak Ridge laboratories were built during World War II, and the national notoriety the town gained during the early days of the Civil Rights movement.

Copies of the book, which one respected Knoxville journalist called "the most professionally-done local history I have seen," now are on the shelves of libraries across the state, providing an example of good interpretation by lay authors and serving as a basis for a local history unit in the Clinton school system. The librarian who headed the Clinton project also proudly reports that the authors still receive requests to speak, the local genealogical society now includes community history in its studies, that individuals, as well as a downtown renovation project, are frequent users of the historic photographs and documents collected during the research phase, and that a videotape of the community's Homecoming '86 pageant, based loosely on their book, is a popular library check-out item.

VALUE AND VALIDITY IN COMMUNITY HERITAGE STUDIES

Communities that received assistance, the Tennessee Humanities Council which sponsored the project, and the Scholars-in-Residence who created and implemented its services and programs share the belief that the project was successful. If measured quantitatively from individual consultations outward to the larger audiences of exhibits, books, radio series, and newspaper inserts, the impact of TCHP is impressive.

As the THC staff pointed out in a subsequent NEH proposal, "the accomplishments of active participants in TCHP-assisted projects soon were perceived to be those of the entire community, the books became best-sellers locally, the exhibits were well-attended, and the workshops led to oral history projects and photographic collections with continuing community value." The TCHP was especially successful at involving people and groups who had been ignored or turned off by more traditional local history studies and organizations, leaving them with real skills for future endeavors. During one TCHP-sponsored discussion, a man in a declining coal-mining community poignantly expressed the need for such on-the-spot assistance: "I have had dealings with state and federal grants for years and in the end they all pass us over in favor of big cities. You're the first ones who have valued us enough to come here to talk."

Despite the apparent success of the TCHP, however, the program was not without problems. One of these was the difficulty of communicating the methods and goals of social history effectively to the lay public. In order to convince the public of the advantages of this approach, the scholars themselves first had to realize, as one stated, "that communities often conceive of heritage projects as social events which trigger reminiscence . . . about something one already knows. . . ." In addition, we sometimes had to deal with unstated community agendas aimed at self-promotion to attract new industry or tourism. By demonstrating, however, how the locality could be fitted into broader cultural and historical contexts, the TCHP scholars were often able to weave valuable analysis and interpretation into what at first glance seemed idiosyncratic or self-serving, or mere "hoopla."

A second major concern for the TCHP was other academicians' lack of interest in consultation, a particularly frustrating problem since we wished to link community groups with university departments and faculty who might assist them after the close of our project. As one TCHP scholar wryly remarked, "Not only did we want to employ them, but we wished to free them from their ivory prisons to share their knowledge with the people. Somebody forgot to tell these scholars that we were coming to free them, or even to ask them if they wanted to be freed." This disinterest can be attributed to inherent problems within the academic domain—teaching overloads, traditional disciplinary foci, or, more significantly, the failure of academic departments, university promotional processes, and professional organizations to treat the work of scholars participating in public humanities programming as professional contribution. The TCHP came then to rely again and again for special consultations upon a small cadre of humanities and social science scholars interested in certain aspects of community or regional studies or, more often, already working outside the mainstream academic setting. A few other professors were willing to give a single lecture, write a short article, or appear in a radio series—activities not too far removed from their normal duties. Graduate students, involved as research assistants, also proved to be a valuable addition in several TCHP-assisted community projects.

Loomis (1983:17) recently suggested that the aim of cultural conservation programs must be to "safeguard and promote community life and values of ethnic, occupational, religious, and regional groups by recovering and protecting treasured patterns that arise from their way of life." Although I agree in spirit with this pronouncement, I also believe that it does not go far enough. The success of the Tennessee Community Heritage Project demonstrates that in order to have long-term and wide-spread benefits, "recovery and protection" must be preceded and accompanied by the active education and involvement of local people in the discovery and interpretation of their own cultural heritage. TCHP was popular because of the same crucial factors Charles Erasmus (1954) associated with giving successful technical assistance in developing nations: TCHP introduced changes which stressed local needs; it was initiated by and through local networks; and it was desireable, effective, and economically feasible. I would suggest that unless professionals include the local populace in cultural conservation as participants and analysts, not just as informants, we ultimately risk our own agendas and resources. Thus, the words of historian Michael Wallace (1987:37) take on multiple levels of meaning for those who hope to conserve and impart the vitality of "old ways" through new methods and interpretations: "People in the past . . . have left us a living matrix of constraints and possibilities within which we must work in the present . . . if we are ignorant of the way our world came into being, we impoverish or even imperil ourselves."

NOTE

1. Funding for the TCHP was provided by the Tennessee Humanities Council, the National Endowment for the Humanities, Lyndhurst Foundation, Hospital Corporation of America, and the state of Tennessee. Although the opinions expressed in this paper are mine, they are based on three years of interaction with the other TCHP Scholars-in-Residence; Dennis Frobish, Jerrold Hirsch, Pat Lane, Wallace Cross, Joanne Taylor, and Robert Gates. Robert Cheatham, Tony Cavender, and Martha Starin of the Tennessee Humanities Council, the board of directors of that organization, and the many community members who participated in TCHP also deserve credit for the project's success.

REFERENCES

Brumberg, David, 1982. The Case for Reunion: Academic Historians, Public Historical Agencies and the New York Historians-In-Residence Program. *Public Historian* 4:89.

Erasmus, Charles J., 1954. An Anthropologist Views Technical Assistance. *Scientific Monthly* 78:147–158.

Hart, Carroll, 1978. Documenting a Vanishing Georgia through Photographs. *Georgia Archive* 6 (1):11–15.

Loomis, Ormond H., coordinator, 1983. *Cultural Conservation: The Protection of Cultural Heritage in the United States* (Washington, D.C.: Library of Congress).

Sand, Viki, 1978. History Resource Units from the Minnesota Historical Society. *American Archivist* 41:163–168.

Wallace, Michael, 1987. The Politics of Public History. In *Past Meets Present: Essays about Historic Interpretation and Public Audiences,* Jo Blatti, ed. (Washington, D.C.: Smithsonian Institution Press).

The Past and the Present: Urban Archaeology in Charleston, South Carolina

Martha A. Zierden

How best to share research with the public is an issue that archaeologists have been wrestling with for a number of years. Archaeologists traditionally have been employed by universities, where they are somewhat removed from the general public. Public interaction became a much-discussed issue with the advent of legal requirements for archaeological excavation preceding federally funded development projects. Cultural resource management (CRM) projects greatly increased the amount of archaeological research conducted in the Southeast, but in many ways this work was even less accessible to the public than conventional grant-sponsored research. Conducted by state and federal agencies, private consulting firms, and universities, CRM projects have tight budgets and deadlines, and the results are reported in technical documents with very limited distribution. Even professional archaeologists are unable to keep up with this growing body of gray literature. Archaeologists in cultural resource management have found it difficult to develop effective outlets for public, or popular, dissemination of archaeological research.

Two recent developments in the field of archaeology are encouraging. The first is the growth of urban archaeology in the United States. Such research programs often focus on a single city, and the archaeologists are employed in some capacity in that municipality. Cities are living sites, whose residents are interested descendants of those being studied. Many urban archaeology programs are designed to explore and preserve the city's heritage and provide links to the present; they have active volunteer, education, publication, and exhibition programs (Bense 1987).

The second new development in the field of archaeology is the employment of archaeologists by small- to medium-sized museums, institutions charged with educating the populace. Such an employment situation provides many opportunities for public involvement. The Charleston Museum's urban archaeology program represents such an endeavor.

Since 1980, the Charleston Museum has sponsored an urban archaeology program in Charleston, South Carolina. The program is designed to combine multidisciplinary research with city and federal goals in protection and preservation to achieve public interaction and education. Using federal, state, city, and private funds, the museum has conducted excavations on twelve urban sites. These projects have employed historians, a zooarchaeologist, ethnobotanist, and educators; an architectural historian and palynologist are recent additions to the team. The results of these projects have been disseminated in standard report form. But by being affiliated with a museum instead of city government or a university, the program has more outlets already in place for public involvement. Interpretations, as well as artifacts, are incorporated into exhibits, ranging from satellite cases located in a variety of public buildings to permanent shows in the main exhibit gallery. In addition to technical reports, small booklets are produced for many projects. Major programs are classes and site visits, offered through the museum's education department, and volunteer programs, including a local archaeological society.

Charleston is a high profile city in which to do archaeology, as the city is extremely proud of its heritage. It was the first in the country to enact protective legislation, as part of a 1931 zoning ordinance; in many ways the city is considered the birthplace of the historic preservation movement. The lower part of the city (138 acres) was established as an Old and Historic District in the 1930s, and the boundaries of this National Register district have been expanded many times (Stoney 1976:134). Charleston is also a favored tourist designation, famous for its stately townhouses and plantations, its heritage of wealth and gracious living, and its role in the Civil War. Charleston now faces the problems and dilemmas of a mature preservation movement (Cohen 1987:32). Interest in, and protection of, archaeological resources is a relatively recent development. One goal of our archaeological program, and of many fine historical studies which have appeared in the past few years, is the "democratization" of the city's history to provide data on the poor and disenfranchised—slaves, free blacks, and white laborers

—who physically built the city, and whose descendants are still part of the community.

We recently had an opportunity to expand our research to include the examination of these disenfranchised groups. This historical research project, funded by the city of Charleston and a matching historic preservation grant administered by the South Carolina Department of Archives and History, was designed to supplement our original research design (Zierden and Calhoun 1984, 1986) by focusing on the development of suburban areas in the nineteenth century and on the history of enslaved and free blacks, who represented a disproportionate percentage of the suburban population. The project had two major goals: to provide a foundation for subsequent archaeological research in the area and to prepare a history of the area that could be used to increase pride in, and knowledge of, the past among present community residents.

A group of patriotic and profit-seeking English noblemen founded the Carolina colony in 1670. In 1680, the Lords Proprietors relocated their first town from a marshy area on Albemarle Point to the more defensible and commercially suitable peninsula formed by the confluence of the Ashley and Cooper rivers (Earle and Hoffman 1977). Here the English settled the area along the Cooper River bounded by present day Water, East Bay, Cumberland, and Meeting Streets. The planned city, known as the Grand Model, was laid out around a central square and divided by wide streets into deep, narrow lots, a plan characteristic of seventeenth-century Irish towns colonized by the British (Reps 1965). While the new Charles Town was a renaissance city in many ways, the surrounding wall and steep roofs gave it a decidedly medieval atmosphere (Coclanis 1984).

As colonists searched for profitable staple crops, the settlement developed gradually as a port and marketing center. An initially successful Indian trade in deer skins provided the impetus for Charles Town's commercial growth. The decade of the 1730s witnessed the town's transformation from a small frontier community to an important mercantile center. When royal rule replaced the inefficient proprietary government in 1729 following a revolt by the settlers, Carolina entered the mainstream of the colonial economy. The development of outlying settlements, following the Township Plan of 1730, brought an influx of products from the back-country. Meanwhile, as rice became more profitable, low-country plantations rapidly expanded. Thousands of Africans were imported as a labor force, and merchants grew rich dealing in staples and slaves. Merchants and planters formed the elite of Charleston society; indeed, the two groups often overlapped, for planters engaged in mercantile endeavors and merchants invested their earnings in land, becoming planters themselves. This strong tie to the country is an important theme in the city's history (Goldfield 1982).

As the eighteenth century advanced, Charles Town expanded in size, economic importance, and the relative affluence of its citizens. White per capita income was among the highest in the colonies (Weir 1983). Still, the city limit remained at Beaufain Street until 1783, when it was moved four blocks north to Boundary Street. Within these confines, a growing population was accommodated by subdividing lots and expanding into the center of blocks. The city was oriented on an east-west axis. In 1783, when the city's name was changed to Charleston, merchants and craftsmen lined the waterfront and three streets, Broad, Tradd, and Elliot, which carried traffic west across the peninsula (Calhoun et al. 1985). Like other eighteenth-century cities, Charleston was a pedestrian town. Merchants needed to be near the waterfront for the sake of convenience as well as for economy of transportation. Hence the area known as Charleston Neck, north of the city proper, was slow to develop.

Africans had arrived as unwilling immigrants with the first Europeans on the shores of the Carolina colony. The topography, climate, and fertility of the low-country was ideal for the production of valuable staples and fostered the development of plantation agriculture. Heat, humidity, and malaria discouraged white settlement (Coclanis 1984; Weir 1983), while the successful production of indigo, rice, and later cotton increased the demand for a labor force (Phillips 1974:8). Besides being accustomed to the subtropical climate, Africans were able to adapt their use of wild foods and natural remedies to the native flora and fauna. Moreover, they possessed skills in rice cultivation and other tasks essential to the plantation (Wood 1975; Littlefield 1981). By 1708, the majority of low-country residents were black. Negro bondsmen and women worked the crops in the countryside and provided labor for building and maintaining the city.

Most slaves were field hands, laborers, servants, or porters, but on plantations and in the city, some served as coopers, blacksmiths, brickmakers, millwrights, carpenters, seamstresses, barbers, fishermen, pastry cooks, and in many other skilled occupations. Owners routinely hired out their Negro artisans. A few slaves won their freedom by buying it; masters manumitted others, especially house servants, in recognition of special skills or services or sometimes in response to familial affection. The emerging class referred to as "free persons of color" congregated in Charleston. In some trades, Negroes displaced white artisans and laborers. All social classes lived side by side in the eighteenth-century city. After 1800, free Negroes and town servants were among the first residents to move to the newly developing boroughs of the Neck, reflecting their growing independence (Berlin 1987). African-Americans constituted a majority of Charleston's population before 1840; by the Civil War, slightly less than one-half of all Charlestonians were black and more than a third of all Charlestonians were slaves (Johnson and Roark 1984:340; Wade 1964:326).

The area of the museum project described here is the East Side, a community now largely black and impoverished. This area is the first encountered by visitors entering the city, and historic restoration and revitalization is moving north from the older city into these nineteenth-century neighborhoods. The East Side is located above Calhoun Street on that portion of the peninsula known as the Neck (see Figure 1). Throughout the colonial era, this area was occupied by plantations and small farms. As the city spread northward, these tracts were subdivided and developed along the lines of English villages (Rogers 1979:580).

The suburbs of the Neck, Hampstead, Mazyckborough, and Wraggsborough, were subdivided and settled in the federal period. Throughout the nineteenth century, the East Side was a mosaic of white, mulatto, and black residents. Wealthy planters chose the spacious breezy lots of the suburbs for their imposing townhouses; some Charleston merchants, manufacturers, attorneys, and physicians built or rented substantial homes in the area. White artisans, tradesmen, and mechanics lived in more modest houses, above shops, or in worker's cottages built by their employers. German and especially Irish immigrants in increasing numbers staked a claim on the Neck, competing for jobs with black people, slave and free.

The Neck had special advantages for city dwellers of African descent, especially for free blacks and for slaves granted the privilege of working and living on their own. Rents were lower, real estate was more available and less expensive, and new houses could be built of wood, a practice discouraged within the city limits. The suburb also offered

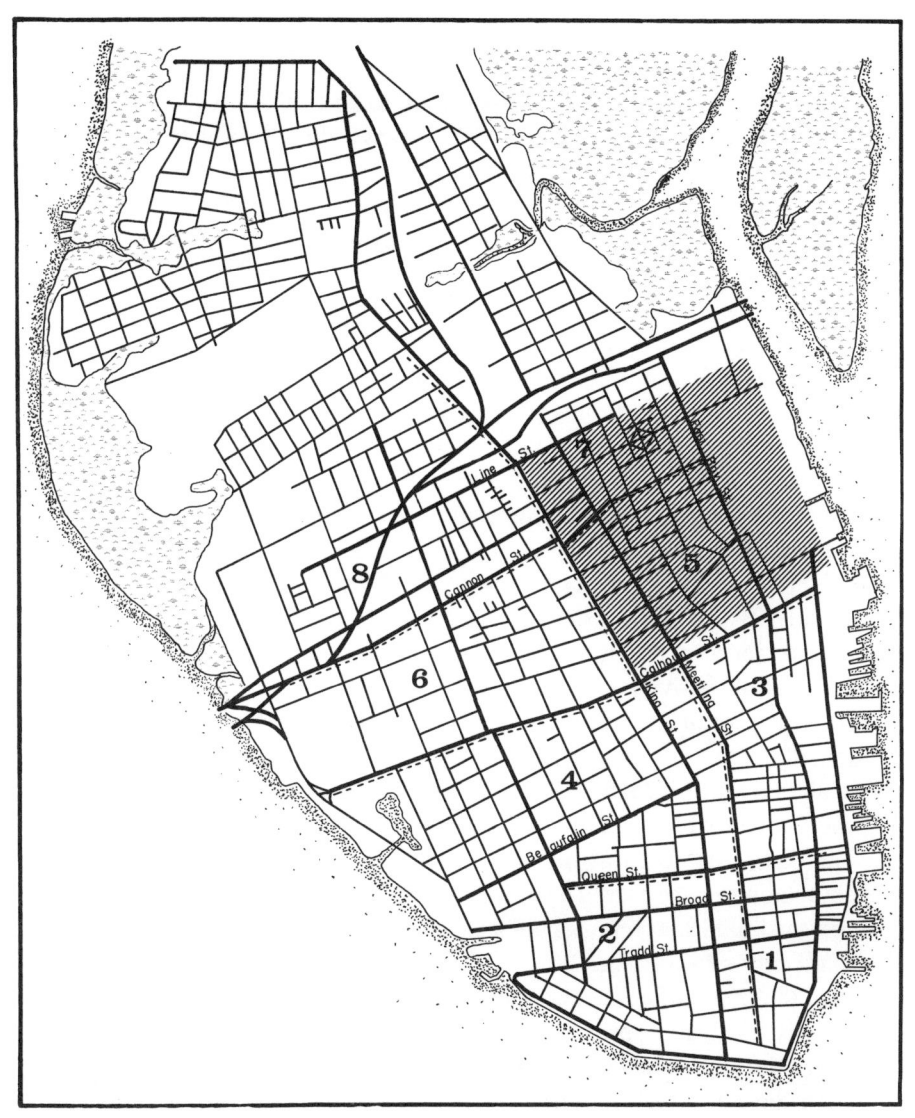

Figure 1
Map of the Charleston peninsula showing the current boundaries of the East Side (shaded area) and the 1850 boundaries of the eight wards

some respite from police surveillance and control; hence the Neck appealed to runaways, slaves "passing as free," and other people eager to expand their personal liberty (Rosengarten et al. 1987:9).

East and west boundaries became more defined as the East Side emerged as the location of choice for Charleston's expanding industries. The South Carolina Railroad and Northeastern Railroad were built between King and Meeting streets and along East Bay street, respectively. Open spaces, lower real estate values, relaxed building restrictions, access to deep water harbors, as well as proximity to the railways attracted large scale manufacturing enterprises. Iron foundries, car manufacturers, and a new gas works were strategically situated between the tracks of the two railroads (Rosengarten et al. 1987:116). In less than half a century, the eastern part of the Neck was transformed from the "country," a sparsely settled suburban haven for planters, to the center of Charleston's industrial future, home to both new industries and their workers.

Unlike the lower city, the East Side recovered from the Civil War quickly. By 1870, war damage had been repaired and new enterprises were underway. The 1880s were likewise characterized by a resurgence in building activity (Rosengarten et al. 1987:27–29). The prosperous and prominent free mulattoes of the antebellum period remained socially elite (Rosengarten et al. 1987:154–155; Koger 1985:190–201; Williamson 1965:316–317), while the emergence of separate black churches provided community cohesion (Williamson 1965:199–200). The district suffered as the city's economy failed to recover from the devastation of the war. The new freedmen continued to work as skilled and unskilled laborers, small-scale merchants, and most prominently as the city's fishermen.

In the first half of the twentieth century, the East Side continued as a racially integrated, primarily working-class community. The economic revitalization of the city during World War I largely bypassed the area. With the advent of automobile transportation and the construction of bridges, white residents flocked to the suburbs. After World War II, portions of the city began to grow more racially segregated. Preservation projects in succeeding decades displaced many black residents, who found new homes north of Calhoun Street. In response to this, the city instituted revitalization/renovation programs to ensure that residents remained in their neighborhood. The city's preservation efforts are now focusing on the East Side, with the goal of keeping the present neighborhoods intact.

Despite the city's sincere efforts to avoid displacement, however, many residents fear gentrification. Such fears are historically grounded. The lovely Ansonborough neighborhood several blocks to the south was once a dilapidated but integrated residential area; it is currently white upper middle class. Especially painful to many older black residents was the razing of black-occupied houses to construct Gaillard Auditorium and the federal building in the 1960s. More recent revitalization efforts suggest that the city has learned from its past mistakes, but East Side residents remain skeptical. The dilemma is embodied in the recent National Register controversy. The state planned to expand the National Register district to include the East Side, and certainly it is a neighborhood worthy of such designation. The citizenry was split over the plan; some felt that such a designation would give the area residents the sense of pride and history that they needed in order to hold onto their homestead; others felt that National Register status, and the accompanying tax credits, would only encourage outside restoration and inflated property values, forcing out lower-income residents, many of whom rent their homes—in other words, inevitable gentrification.

The mixed feelings of community residents are embodied in the following quotes that were printed in our small booklet. Philip Simmons, nationally famous blacksmith (see Vlach 1981) and long-time East Side resident, suggests: "This was the first area that the free slave lived in and I would want to come back tomorrow and see that we preserved what they left. I think we must become part of the National Register, otherwise I feel like we are going to be pushed off, not a part of this Charleston beauty." Lorraine Fordham, childhood resident of the East Side and a descendant of the Dereefs, a socially prominent free black family, feels otherwise: "I have feelings both ways, but I think the con would outweigh the pro. I'm thinking of all these black people who will be displaced, which I feel is sure to come."

It was on the heels of this controversy that the museum was awarded the East Side Survey grant. Largely ignorant of the controversy, we were initially surprised to encounter resistance to the project by leaders of the black community; their rancor was aimed not at us, but at the city. This was seen as just another move to encourage outside development and to ignore the feelings and desires of the populace.

This potentially negative situation was also a major opportunity for the museum. Recently rebuilt on the East Side, the Charleston Museum had an opportunity to become part of its own neighborhood, to emerge as a leader in local black history research. A steering committee of community leaders, city representatives, and black scholars was formed. Initially skeptical, these people soon became enthusiastically involved in the project and were our liason with the community. An oral history component was added at the request of the neighborhood representatives, and the Avery Research Center for Afro-American history and culture, under the direction of Myrtle Glascoe, became a co-worker in the project.

What I had envisioned as a basic research project became a public history project. The steering committee met on several occasions, read each of the several drafts of the project report and booklet, and provided the names of local informants. They also suggested topics of local interest, such as the Mosquito Fleet, for further research.[1] The resulting written report and accompanying booklet were distributed free to the East Side residents by steering committee members. The public history project then became the foundation for long-term African-American research, sponsored by the museum, Avery Research Center, and the city of Charleston. Controlled archaeological excavations and public education programs were seen as the next step. These two goals were recently combined in a single project, through a new and innovative program. The Preservation Craftsmanship Program is the combined effort of Burke High School, a predominantly black high school on the West Side, and Historic Charleston Foundation. This vocational program is designed to teach students the skills needed to restore old homes. Workers possessing these skills, such as plaster work and brick pointing, are becoming hard to find, and these students will possess marketable skills perfected by their forefathers—slave and free black bricklayers and carpenters. The program is directed by a man of unquenchable energy, Assistant Principal Vince Lannie. He feels that, in addition to manual skills, the students should be exposed to every aspect of historic restoration, including site planning, historical research, archaeological excavation, and community history. To this end, we conducted a small archaeological testing program on an East Side property. Number 14 Amherst street has been purchased by Historic Charleston Foundation for restoration, and the Preservation Craftsmanship students will participate in its renovation. The site currently looks insignificant, but it dates to the late eighteenth century and is one of the earliest structures in the area.

Students began the archaeological project with a slide lecture on archaeological methods. This was followed by a one-day shovel testing of the small side yard. Students participated in every aspect of the excavation, from grid layout to digging and screening. Then they reconvened in the lab to wash, sort, and identify excavated materials. Another aspect of the program was a walking tour of the East Side neighborhood. The full semester of classes was followed by a spring semester of internship and on-the-job training. During the second year, the students will be employed by area restoration carpenters for pay. Plans call for archaeological research to remain an integral part of this program.

Today, community pride among East Side residents is increasing. A new post office is a welcome addition, as are a variety of city projects. These include the East Side Community Center, located in the remodeled 1902 incinerator, and the Business and Technology Center, located in the revitalized 1880s Tobacco Factory. The East Side Neighborhood Council will offer a variety of self-help services as well as exhibits on the history of the neighborhood in a restored corner store, renovated with assistance from the city. The exhibits were developed with the guidance of the museum.

Community Development funds are used for a variety of housing improvement projects. The city spent four million dollars to rehabilitate 245 East Side units between 1975 and 1986. These federal, municipal, and private monies are administered through a variety of programs, including rental housing rehabilitation, emergency repair, paint program, urban homesteading, and the homeownership program. Important new programs include the owner-occupied loan/grant program and section 312 program. Most exciting is the innovative housing program. Instead of large, unsightly "projects," the city is constructing small apartment buildings in the style of the famous Charleston single house (an architectural style unique to the low-country). These structures improve the neighborhood by adding an attractive and architecturally appropriate building to a vacant lot. They also disperse low-income housing throughout the existing neighborhood (hence the nickname "scattered housing"), avoiding the visible stigma associated with large housing projects. Forty-six such units are located on twelve East Side sites; these projects have won Presidential and National Endowment for the Arts design awards (Cohen 1987:38).

New leaders are emerging who promote the history and heritage of the community. We were fortunate to have some of these individuals on our steering committee, and interaction with them has continued since completion of the research project. This facilitates continued museum-community interaction.

It remains to be seen if the good intentions of the city, grass-roots community programs, and the sense of place provided by archaeological and historical research will be sufficient to overcome the basic laws of economy and forestall gentrification. The preliminary research projects discussed here indicate that such studies are important to the black community. The data generated by documentary research, and especially archaeological excavations, are greatly expanding knowledge of the African-American contribution to the city's heritage. Further, public participation in the acquisition of that knowledge will hasten the preservation of the fragile artifacts of that history. Especially important are projects that allow children and young adults physically and tangibly to explore and preserve their heritage. "The East Side has historically been a place where there's lots of good people" says Arthur K. Maybank, president of the East Side Neighborhood Council. "We're trying to show how a neighborhood can help itself."

NOTE

1. The Mosquito Fleet was a group of black fishermen who daily sailed their small boats offshore to the blackfish banks. They were the primary suppliers of fresh fish to the Charleston market in the nineteenth and twentieth centuries and are still active on a limited basis.

REFERENCES

Bense, Judith, 1987. Developing a Management System for Archaeological Resources in Pensacola, Florida. In *Living in Cities,* Edward Staski, ed. (Special Publication 5, Society for Historical Archaeology), pp. 83–91.

Berlin, Ira, 1987. Part 2: The Making of Americans. *American Visions* 2(2): 14–21.

Calhoun, Jeanne, Martha Zierden, and Elizabeth Paysinger, 1985. The Geographic Spread of Charleston's Mercantile Community, 1732–1767. *South Carolina Historical Magazine* 86(3):182–220.

Coclanis, Peter A., 1984. Economy and Society in the Early Modern South: Charleston and the Evolution of the South Carolina Lowcountry (Ph.D. diss., Columbia University).

Cohen, Daniel, 1987. Charleston's Restoration Challenge. *Historic Preservation* 39(1):30–39.

Earle, Carville, and Ronald Hoffman, 1977. The Urban South: The First Two Centuries. In *The City in Southern History,* Blaine Brownell and David Goldfield, eds. (Port Washington, N.Y.: Kennikat Press), pp. 23–51.

Goldfield, David R., 1982. *Cotton Fields and Skyscrapers: Southern City and Region, 1607–1980* (Baton Rouge: Louisiana State University Press).

Johnson, Michael P., and James L. Roark, 1984. *Black Masters: A Free Family of Color in the Old South* (New York: W. W. Norton and Company).

Koger, Larry, 1985. *Black Slaveowners: Free Black Masters in South Carolina, 1790–1860* (Jefferson, N.C.: McFarland and Company).

Littlefield, Daniel, 1981. *Rice and Slaves: Ethnicity and the Slave Trade in Colonial South Carolina* (Baton Rouge: Louisiana State University Press).

Phillips, U. B., 1974. The Slave Labor Problem in the Charleston District. In *Plantation, Town, and County,* Elinor Miller and Eugene Genovese, eds. (Urbana: University of Illinois Press), pp. 7–28.

Reps, John, 1965. *The Making of Urban America: A History of City Planning in the United States* (Princeton, N.J.: Princeton University Press).

Rogers, George C., David R. Chestnutt, and Peggy J. Clark, eds., 1979. *The Papers of Henry Laurens, Volume 7: August 1, 1769–October 9, 1771* (Columbia: University of South Carolina Press).

Rosengarten, Dale, et al., 1987. *Between the Tracks: Charleston's East Side during the Nineteenth Century.* Archaeological Contributions 17 (Charleston, S.C.: Charleston Museum).

Stoney, Samuel Gaillard, 1976. *This is Charleston: An Architectural Survey of a Unique American City* (Charleston, S.C.: Carolina Art Association).

Vlach, John M., 1981. *Charleston Blacksmith: The Work of Philip Simmons* (Athens: University of Georgia Press).

Wade, Richard C., 1964. *Slavery in the Cities: The South, 1820–1860* (New York: Oxford University Press).

Weir, Robert M., 1983. *Colonial South Carolina: A History* (Millwood, N.Y.: KTO Press).

Williamson, Joel, 1965. *After Slavery: The Negro in South Carolina Dur-*

ing Reconstruction, 1861–1877 (Chapel Hill: University of North Carolina Press).

Wood, Peter H., 1975. *Black Majority: Negroes in Colonial South Carolina from 1670 through the Stono Rebellion* (New York: Alfred A. Knopf).

Zierden, Martha and Jeanne Calhoun, 1984. An Archaeological Preservation Plan for Charleston, South Carolina. Archaeological Contributions 8 (Charleston, S.C.: Charleston Museum).

——, 1986. Urban Adaptation in Charleston, South Carolina, 1730–1820. *Historical Archaeology* 20(1): 29–43.

Appalshop: Preserving, Participating in, and Creating Southern Mountain Culture

Helen M. Lewis

Appalshop, a media center in Whitesburg, Kentucky, began as an Office of Economic Opportunity job training project for Appalachian youth in 1969. Several community film workshops were developed during the War on Poverty to train poor and minority youth in the skills of film and television production with the hope that they could find jobs in the television and film industry. The Eastern Kentucky workshop was the rural Appalachian workshop, located in the Central Appalachian coal fields, which was the locus of many poverty programs of the sixties. Young high school students were attracted to the storefront workshop, and they soon began filming basketball games, car races, and interviews with other young people about their dreams and hopes for the future. They also began interviewing their neighbors and kinfolk to document their "mountain ways."

Employment opportunities were beginning to decline in the urban industrial areas when the training was over or the funds were cut off; most of the young people decided they would prefer to remain at home. So a group of the young people trained in the workshop incorporated as Appalshop, a not-for-profit media arts center, and began creating their own jobs. The work they were doing documenting the culture of their own community made them value their home more. Herb Smith, one of the first filmmakers, said: "We began to learn about our own place . . . a lot of valuable things about our home. Once we learned who we were, who our people were, and more about the place that we were a part of, then we wanted to stay. We began to try to figure out how could we stay here without going into the coal mines, how could we create an alternative organization where we could be a positive force in the region."

Other young people in the region joined the group, and by 1975 Appalshop had grown to include Appalshop Films, Roadside Theater, June Appal Recordings, *Mountain Review,* and Mountain Photography Workshop. In 1979, the television series "Headwaters" began broadcasting from Hazard, Kentucky. In 1982, the organization completed renovation of the Appalshop building, a thirteen thousand square foot production, distribution, and exhibition facility in downtown Whitesburg. In 1985 WMMT-FM, a community radio station, began operation. Appalshop grew from a training center with one full-time employee in 1969 to an artist-run production center with an annual budget of $240,000 in 1977. Since then Appalshop has expanded into a regional cultural center with more than thirty full-time employees and an annual budget in excess of one million dollars.

By looking at the films, one can trace some of the changes in the region and the growth and changes in consciousness of the filmmakers. *Woodrow Cornett: Letcher County Butcher* (1971) was the first film completed, a ten-minute black-and-white portrait of a country butcher, a straightforward account of a country hog-killing. It shows the style which became a trademark of Appalshop: simple, matter of fact, straightforward, without fancy techniques. It is the story, without outside interpretation, of how people get their food; but it says much about skill, tradition, self-sufficiency, and production. Many films that followed show the old-time, traditional forms of work: farming, chairmaking, bartering and trading, running a grist mill, or making whiskey. Tradition was early defined by Appalshop as more than romantic mountain lifestyle with dulcimers and cornshuck dolls; it included ways of making a living and patterns of subsistence and survival.

Another early film, *In Ya Blood* (1971) is a docudrama which Herb Smith, just out of high school himself, directed and edited. He also played the central role of Randy, a young man broke, in love, needing a car, loving the mountains, but facing a big decision: whether to leave the mountains for college, if he can find the money, or stay and work in the coal mines. The love-hate relation with coal-mining and the problems it has brought to the mountains, as well as the love of the mountains and the pushes and pulls to leave, are themes often repeated in later Appalshop films.

One of Appalshop's first major projects was funded by the National Endowment for the Arts and involved further training in filmmaking and preservation of Appalachian culture. New recruits learned filmmaking by making films, and they made a series which included a film of the Old Regular Baptist Church, chairmakers, basketmakers, traditional musicians, cock-fighting, an old grist mill, quilters, and mountain farmers. In these films they developed their art and style and learned from the people they interviewed. Their style was to let people tell their own story without interjecting their analysis and to allow the subject matter to speak for itself with a minimum of interference from the filmmaker. The films are laced with humor and play even when they deal with poverty and tragedy. You become aware that the people are friends and neighbors, often kinfolk, and you are aware that the creators of the films are themselves part of the culture they are recording. In combination, the filmmakers and the subjects are producing the film together, going beyond stereotypes to see the person in context. They are not only documenting, but participating in and creating their own culture.

There were serious social and economic problems and major conflicts going on in the mountains. The filmmakers began struggling with how to address these issues and also live with the controversy they produced. They made films about strip-mining, coal mine disasters, women in the mines, union reform, coal strikes, environmental problems, tobacco farming, and politics. One of the first of these controversial films was made by a young student intern from California, Mimi Pickering, who was working in West Virginia and sought Appalshop's help in making a film about a community fighting school consolidation. Again by letting people tell their stories and coming down on the side of those who were hurt, oppressed, exploited, and fighting against the injustices, Pickering portrayed the people not as poor and pitiful, but proud, courageous, and determined to make changes.

The filmmakers were not heavy crusaders but documented the struggles and problems, and the traditional forms of resistance and solutions which people had worked out. This pattern has continued. It allows the community to tell its story and provides them with a film to use in their struggle. In this way Appalshop has become an important resource to the many grass roots groups in the mountains trying to change the economic and political situation. But this role has not been without difficulties and conflicts, because the community and families are polarized around the issues. Since her first film, Mimi Pickering joined Appalshop and has made a number of films dealing with important issues: *The Buffalo Creek Flood: An Act of Man* (1975), *Buffalo Creek Revisited* (1984), and current film projects on the chemical industry in West Virginia and on Sarah Ogan Gunning, a protest singer-songwriter from the Harlan County union organizing days of the thirties. Appalshop also made other kinds of films, such as interviews with artists and writers, including Jean Ritchie, James Still, and Harriette Arnow.

In the late 1970s, a new series of films on the history of the region was begun. I joined the staff in 1980 to work with the filmmakers to develop this series. In the beginning the major goal was writing and rewriting the history of the region, a neglected part of history. We meant to fill in the blank spaces, dispel stereotypes, and tell the history from the viewpoint of the people who experienced it. As we researched, scripted, and looked for the context, patterns, or themes around which we could develop the film series, we began to better understand the region as part of national and international history. Instead of just dispelling stereotypes, we wanted to present Appalachia as a microcosm of national and international changes. For example, the second film, *Long Journey Home* (1987), changed from a simple look at the diversity of population (not just pure Anglo-Saxon) to a history of migrations. We found that we wanted to do more than just rewrite history. We were seeking to develop a synthesis, presenting the region as part of American history and as part of changes going on in the world.

Academics frequently act as humanities scholars for film projects to bring a humanities perspective and build a bridge between academia and the community. There are problems, disadvantages which academics have in working with media; one is being tied to the written word. But there is an important role for academics in conceptualizing social relations, helping to define and analyze cultural patterns. Sociologists and anthropologists have certain disadvantages in working with historical film, especially their own lack of adequate historical knowledge. Our advantage is that we are not afraid to generalize, use "cases" to represent a large body of knowledge, and use fiction and oral histories, people's stories, and myths to show how people perceive their situations. We look to social relations, themes of the times, ideologies. But like most academics we are also tied to the written word and need to be reeducated, to develop visual literacy.

During the research and development of the history series, we formed a large network of regional scholars, writers, oral historians, and other resource people who worked closely with the filmmakers throughout the process. In addition to an advisory committee who advised and monitored the total process, we sought special consultants for each film with expertise in fields such as demography, migration, Cherokee history, geology, religion, and music. The process that we developed for the cooperation of filmmakers, regional scholars, and researchers was exciting and productive. By studying, researching, discussing together the nature of the region, the forces of change, the conflicts and dilemmas faced by mountain people, we developed a much better understanding of our history. The process was educational for both scholars and filmmakers and resulted in an interesting and constructive dialogue. The filmmakers and writers learned much from the academic scholars, and the scholars learned to look at history and their field of expertise more visually.

The first film, *Strangers and Kin* (1984), dealt with the history of images and stereotypes. The filmmakers felt that first they had to look at how the people and the area had been portrayed and the reasons why. The original plan was for a seven-film series, but Reagan budget cuts and new guidelines at the National Endowment for the Humanities, which eliminated the focus on regional history, resulted in the series being dropped by the National Endowment after the first film. The second film was funded by a coalition of state humanities councils.

In its research, scripting, and working with scholars, the history series was much more ambitious than earlier films, yet it incorporated Appalshop style: retell the history of the region from the viewpoint of the people and in traditional storytelling style. *Strangers and Kin* used dramatizations of historical statements about the region by Appalshop's theater group, Roadside Theater, and mixed archival pictures, documentary films, and Hollywood and television images to tell the history of stereotypes, how they came into being, and how the storytellers felt about them.

The film *Strangers and Kin* resulted in controversy, aroused emotions, and stimulated debate. It angered some who objected to the way the film questioned "progress," and it irritated others who resented its not giving clear answers to the dilemma of modernization and tradition. It helped us better understand how to use film to bring about debate and dialogue about these changes and the basic issues of our age. We tried to look at the reactions to this film to better understand what film can do that written history does not. Films can present emotional experiences so that one understands emotionally as well as, or maybe instead of, logically and intellectually. Historical information and political and philosophical arguments are probably better expressed in debate and written words. Films are not good at being objective. But films are better at showing the feelings of people in certain times, places, and situations, showing the emotions related to events. But because films show emotions they also raise emotions in the audience.

Appalshop filmmakers never have been objective observers. As they have documented Appalachian history and culture through film, video, music recordings, theater, photography, and radio, they have been an important part of the cultural revitalization movement in the Appalachian region in 1970s and 1980s. They have been both participants and creators as well as documenting and preserving regional culture. Appalshop has been part of a cultural revival in the mountains and like *Foxfire* has helped rediscover and reinterpret Appalachia for its generation.

The staff has attracted people from outside the area but it largely consists of people locally born and raised. Many of those who were the first trainees and set the style and philosophy of Appalshop were also influenced by 1960s politics and alternative culture; they were leaders in the Appalachian Movement of the 1970s, and they added an anti-elitist, egalitarian stamp to their interpretation of history and culture. Even in portraying a mountain artist to document some of the more traditional, isolated culture of older, rural Appalachians, they also sought out activist-traditionalists (*Nimrod Workman: To Fit My Own Category*, 1975), or old-time hippies (*Catfish Man of the Woods*, 1974), or artists like Chester Cornett (*Chairmaker*, 1975) who had coped with modernization. They early became critics of modernization, yet at the same time were part of and endorsed the new alternative lifestyles and politics alongside the "good old-fashioned way." They saw how in many ways new alternatives were similar in values and style to traditional ways. Both made strong statements—criticisms of modern industrial life and an exploitative economic system.

Because the Appalshop staff have endorsed change as well as been strong proponents of preserving traditional culture, they have been criticized by traditional folklorists, especially in their music recording program. They have recorded many revivalist musicians, young mountain blues artists, and young mountain composers as well as older traditional musicians. They claim to record the best of mountain music, old and new, insisting that mountain culture is not static, but alive, growing, and changing. They see no contradictions between recording young mountain folks writing and playing new mountain music and portraying the Old Regular Baptists singing at the riverside baptism. Both are part of the culture.

From the beginning, Appalshop had to deal with local issues and problems, some of crisis proportions, such as the Buffalo Creek flood, and others very controversial, such as strip-mining (*Strip Mining in Appalachia*, 1973; *Strip Mining: Energy, Environment & Economics*, 1979). Members had to deal with their own families, some of whom worked as coal miners and others who were coal operators. Their reputation as radical hippies in a small mountain town led to family conflicts, lots of gossip, and estrangements from the establishment. Many people in Whitesburg were suspicious of the long-haired young people running around with cameras and microphones, asking all kinds of questions. Now these young people are parents and approaching middle-age. The institution is important to the economy of the area. Appalshop has a new building and a set of forty films, videos, records, and plays which portray the region differently from national media. Appalshop has won the approval of most of its neighbors, although the coal industry still avoids the group if possible.

From the beginning the group operated as a collective, and its style of operation is interesting and successful. It has become somewhat more professional and less anarchic but without the formal hierarchical structure which eliminates the emotional and personal. Appalshop has successfully dealt with both personal and professional issues as a workers' board made up of neighbors, friends, and, sometimes, adversaries.

As "native" filmmakers and scholars, we are the cultural insiders, participants and agents of the history we seek to define and analyze. We are not only studying and presenting the images of the region, but we are redefining in our own terms what the region and the history are, and how people who live here have been affected by the history. We try to present it fairly and lovingly. We experience tension as we use high-tech electronic media to show traditional culture and the dilemmas which Appalachians faced from the beginning: how to enter or remain part of the national and international marketplace and American culture, how to deal with modernization and technological change and still preserve "community" and the traditional cultural bonds which are antagonistic to such modernization and industrial development. This dilemma has been faced by mountain people each generation. They cannot avoid change, but the main question is who controls it. Appalshop works to be part of and legitimize people's attempts to control their own development and maintain community and tradition.

REFERENCES

The Buffalo Creek Flood: An Act of Man. 1975. 40 min. Black and white, 16mm and video. Mimi Pickering, director.
Buffalo Creek Revisited. 1984. 31 min. Color, 16mm and video. Mimi Pickering, director.
Catfish Man of the Woods. 1974. 27 min. Color, 16mm and video. Alan Bennett, director.
Chairmaker. 1975. 22 min. Color, 16mm and video. Rick DiClemente, director.
In Ya Blood. 1971. 20 min. Black and white, 16mm and video. Herb E. Smith, director.
Long Journey Home. 1987. 58 min. Color, 16mm and video. Elizabeth Barret, director.
Nimrod Workman: To Fit My Own Category. 1975. 35 min. Black and white, 16mm and video. Scott Faulkner and Anthony Slone, directors.
Strangers and Kin. 1984. 58 min. Color, 16mm and video. Herb E. Smith, director.
Strip Mining: Energy, Environment & Economics. 1979. 50 min. Color, 16mm and video. Frances Morton and Gene Dubey, directors.
Strip Mining in Appalachia. 1973. 29 min. Black and white, 16mm and video. Gene Dubey, director.
Woodrow Cornett: Letcher County Butcher. 1971. 10 min. Black and white, 16mm. Bill Richardson and Frank Majority, directors.

Catface Country: A Case Study in Cultural Conservation

Roger G. Branch and Richard Persico, Jr.

The folk festival is as American as apple pie; indeed, there probably is an apple pie festival somewhere. This prominent feature of popular culture can also serve as a particularly appropriate and effective vehicle for cultural conservation. To varying degrees many folk festivals by their very character and content fulfill this function as a matter of course. Those which focus on regional or ethnic lifeways are obvious examples. In other cases the folk theme serves mainly as a come-on in a fun-for-profit venture.

The Catface Country Turpentine Festival is perhaps unique in that the festival was created to serve as a vehicle for cultural conservation. It blends the efforts of "old-timers" steeped in the lore of turpentining and social scientists with interests and academic expertise in the field. A living artifact in the form of a working turpentine still, a museum, a documentary film, and unobtrusive lectures in the guise of free-form dialogue between experts and members of the crowd—these are prominent features in this on-going project which integrates education and cultural conservation in a folk festival. Of course, typical festival features are included: arts and crafts, parades, speeches, clowns, and kiddie rides. These activities, along with the interesting character of the educational components, make for palatable and effective cultural transmission. What follows is something of an ethnography of the project.

CATFACE COUNTRY: THE WORLD OF TURPENTINING

The extraction and processing of pine resin was one of the earliest industries in colonial North America. Tar and pitch, produced by burning pine logs, were used in those days of wooden sailing ships to caulk seams and preserve rope rigging. Consequently, the name naval stores was applied to this industry. Such was the demand for naval stores in Great Britain, the largest maritime power of the era, that production was attempted in almost all of the North American colonies.

The vast pine forests of North Carolina soon became the center of the naval stores industry. In the plantation areas, tar production was a source of winter work for the slaves, while in the less fertile "pine barrens" it provided the settlers' chief source of income. Backwoods families not only burned deadwood for tar during the winter but also wounded living trees and collected the resin or gum which ran from them during the warmer months. Gradually, the market for gum grew and its production became more profitable. This attracted the attention of plantation owners who began to establish camps in the deep pine woods where groups of slaves extracted the gum.

Early methods of extraction were very destructive of timber; the industry gradually spread south and west into Georgia, Alabama, and Louisiana in search of healthy, untapped trees. Following the Civil War, the woods work shifted from slave labor to work by freed men; but the system of debt peonage bound the laborers, most of whom were black, to their employers almost as effectively as had slavery. As demand for distilled gum spirits of turpentine and rosin grew during the late nineteenth and early twentieth centuries, the numbers of turpentine camps kept pace. After World War II, however, less expensive substitutes for gum products became increasingly available and the cost of labor rose, cutting into the profitability of the industry. New labor laws, improvements in civil rights for blacks, and increased mobility of the workforce all adversely affected turpentining. At present, few full-time producers remain. The turpentine camp is all but a thing of the past. For much of Southern history, and especially during the period from the 1870s through the 1950s, however, turpentining was a major Southern industry, and isolated, virtually self-contained turpentine camps were a prominent feature in Southern pine forests. Their isolation and the nature of the industry which generated them were important factors in producing a Southern subculture in which both black workers and white owners and managers participated.

Located deep in the pine forest, a typical turpentine camp was isolated from neighboring communities by distance, bad roads, and poor sources of transportation.[1] Physically, it centered around two major structures, the commissary building and the distillery. The commissary was the company store, supplying the workers and their families with staples on credit. It also usually served as the front office of the operation where the books were kept and the payroll calculated. The work day started and ended on the commissary porch with the men picking up a few things for lunch in the morning and for supper when their day's work was done. Often it was also the place where errant workers received their reprimands for serious offenses.

The distillery was the ultimate source of income for the entire camp. Here skilled distillers converted the raw gum collected by the woods workers into marketable commodities, turpentine and rosin. The still was a somewhat hazardous place, since pine gum and turpentine are highly combustible and distilled turpentine vapors even more volatile.

Near these two structures were the houses for the families of the owner or manager and the woodsriders. These people were usually white and, in the segregated South, their homes were set apart from the houses of the black workers. The workers' houses, known as "the quarters," were small but typically well kept. Most families grew gardens nearby. Water was typically drawn from communal wells and electricity was not available until very recently. Often a house would be provided to serve as a church and sometimes as a school. Frequently another vacant house would serve as a "juke joint," a site for drinking, gambling, music, and dancing.

The production of gum required a great deal of labor. A large operation might employ between one hundred and two hundred woods workers. The work itself varied from season to season, and a distinctive jargon evolved for the various tools and tasks. From spring through early fall while the pine sap flowed, men engaged in *chipping, pulling,* and *dipping*. These terms refer to the process of wounding a tree and collecting the gum which flowed from the wound. They used a *hack* or a *puller* to chip a *bark streak,* while a *cup cover* kept the chips out of the gum being collected in a cup at the base of the *streak*. The *dipper* used a *dip iron* to collect the gum which he took to the *dip barrels* on the mule-drawn *bunch wagon,* which he used to haul the gum to the *bunch ground*. During the colder months, the work shifted to *punching scrape* and then still later to *hanging virgin*. This meant scraping the dried gum off the scarred faces (*catfaces*) of trees at the end of the season and then preparing new trees to be tapped during the coming spring. This jargon also extended to many other familiar objects and activities. A worker might eat a *dooby* for lunch at the *hang up ground,* play a game of *skin* in the evening, drink some *low wine* from the still if he felt bad, or *juke* all night if he felt good. As is true in most subcultures, familiarity with the jargon was an important symbolic indicator of membership in the group.

While the men worked in the woods, their wives cared for the children, maintained their homes, and worked to supplement the family income. Almost every family raised a portion of its food by gardening and raising some pigs and chickens. Some of the women and children also gathered and dried deertongue, an aromatic plant used in cigars and cigarettes, during the appropriate season. Buyers came to the camps periodically to collect the harvest.

The distillery workers were the elite of the turpentine camp. The stiller himself was the most skilled worker. Under his direction, the raw pine gum was loaded into the copper still vat, mixed with water, and boiled to evaporate the spirits of turpentine. These were collected and cooled in a huge copper coil condenser, called a *worm,* which was immersed in a water-filled tank to speed the condensation. When all of the turpentine had been extracted from the gum, the residue was drawn off, filtered, and allowed to cool into solid rosin. Both turpentine and rosin were sold. At times, rosin brought a better price than the turpentine.

Despite all of their labor, most of the turpentine workers were in debt to their employers most of the time. Debt was often used to keep workers from shifting jobs in areas where the demand for labor was high. If a producer was willing to allow a worker to move, he would collect the outstanding debt from the worker's new employer so that he began his new job already in debt.

The physical isolation of the turpentine camps, a product of poor transportation and the need for workers to live deep in the pine woods, was further enhanced by social isolation. Turpentiners were able to go into the local towns only infrequently. When they did so, it was a cause for celebration. Pent-up energy and surplus cash were spent in one or two nights of enthusiastic partying. Fights with fists or knives were not uncommon. This gave turpentiners, both workers and producers, reputations as wild and tough men. The camps, likewise, were considered dangerous places. Many of the turpentiners apparently relished their "tough guy" reputations. Nevertheless, this further contributed to their isolation and enhanced their identity as a distinct group within rural Southern society.

GENESIS OF THE PROJECT

Denver Hollingsworth was the father of the Catface Country Festival. He is a native of the region and an ardent preservationist. Early products of his energy and commitment were the Bulloch County (Georgia) Historical Society and the assembling of a rudimentary village of restored nineteenth-century buildings—a church, one-room school, etc., on the historical society's grounds. He is a tireless and tenacious zealot for the preservation of salient aspects of the daily lives of plain people of his region, with particular focus upon the late nineteenth and early twentieth centuries.

In 1982, Hollingsworth turned his attention to an old dream as yet unfulfilled, the restoration of a turn-of-the century type fire still to operating condition. The best candidate, the one requiring the least reconstruction and the most readily accessible, was in Portal, Georgia, a village of about one thousand people. Hollingsworth had lived nearby in the country during part of his childhood, had attended school there, remembered the still in the heyday of its operation, and knew by full name and family lineage almost everyone in town. The still had been built and operated by F. N. Carter, Sr., and his family. His sons Earnest C. and F. N., Jr., listened to the restoration scheme with skepticism, then interest, then enthusiasm. Operating mainly with donated materials, volunteer labor, and boundless optimism, Hollingsworth set out to repair and rebuild the facility and he did it.

Assured of the realization of his dream of restoring the still, Hollingsworth turned to Roger Branch, the senior author of this article, for help with the more important dream. What he really wanted was to use the restored still as an instrument for teaching a new generation of south Georgians and others about turpentining as a part of the history and lifeways of much of the South. Hollingsworth was acquainted with Branch's work on cultural heritage projects, especially some supported by the National Endowment for the Humanities and the Georgia Endowment for the Humanities. In addition to his strong interest in the cultural heritage of the region and the "insider" insights of a native, Branch was seen as a useful resource person because he was part of a loosely organized Cultural Heritage Team from the faculty of Georgia Southern College. The team was, and is, composed of anthropologists, sociologists, and historians, with occasional involvements of others based on interest. Their commitment to educational outreach in the area and their interest and expertise in local history and culture made them invaluable resources for a project in cultural conservation.

To achieve the goal of teaching large numbers of people about the history and culture of the world of turpentining, two basic, coordinated approaches were adopted by Hollingsworth, Branch, and Larry Platt, a specialist in research, community development, and grants. The first was an educational project which included seminars, exhibits, a keynote address, and a documentary film. Staffed by a multidisciplinary team drawn mainly from the faculty of Georgia Southern College, this project was funded through a grant from the Georgia Endowment for the Humanities. The second approach was to launch a folk festival. It was intended to reach a large, diverse audience, most of whom would not be attracted to the more formal educational features.

The formal project was divided into two phases, the first taking place in the Conference Center of Georgia Southern College and the second fifteen miles away at the still site in Portal. The first involved presentations and discussions on local history and culture, especially as related to turpentining, regional literature, and art; an exhibit of turpentining tools and artifacts; an exhibit of regional art; and a keynote address by the president of the American Turpentine Farmers Association. One of the highlights was the showing of the documentary film "Spirits of the Pines" with commentary by Gaynell G. Wright, an anthropologist whose ethnographic work provided the inspiration for the film. She also appeared prominently in the film as interviewer. Another was the exhibit of turpentining artifacts.

While the first phase was well attended and well liked, the project's most innovative aspects took place at the still site. The exhibit became a small museum, arranged and staffed by Richard Persico, Sue Moore, and Tim Moore, the latter two archaeologists with expertise in artifact preparation and curation. The film-plus-commentary feature also was moved to the still site and was presented continuously throughout the afternoon. Frank Saunders, a native of the community and a specialist in local history, was joined by colleagues George Rogers, Ray

Shurbutt, and by Branch and Platt in a novel educational tactic. Circulating through the crowd, they engaged small groups and individuals in conversations which in fact instructed people about turpentining, its history, associated lifeways, and the distillation process. These on-site activities were repeated on the second day of the festival, which, as anticipated, attracted large crowds.

Hollingsworth, who had founded the Mill Creek Arts and Crafts Festival and guided it for a decade, directed efforts to begin the turpentine festival. He was joined by a small, varied, and committed group of Portal citizens who brought with them the diverse skills and dedication necessary to meet a daunting challenge. An ad hoc organization was created and committees were assigned to handle various aspects of the festival. From the outset its basic educational goals were articulated and emphasized. To encourage attendance it was decided that no admission fee would be charged. Broad community participation by school groups and churches was encouraged. By festival day the sleepy little town had come alive with civic pride—cleaned up, trimmed up, and ready.

It all came together on October 16 and 17, 1982. The people of Portal in partnership with a team of anthropologists, sociologists, and historians created a festival which was a unique medium of cultural conservation. Total attendance for the two days was seven thousand, according to police estimates. People saw the old still fired for the first time in almost half a century. Old men sparked new interest and respect in their children and grandchildren as they told about "how we used to do it" around the museum and still. It worked.

FURTHER DEVELOPMENTS

Good beginnings guarantee nothing about the future. An important next step was to move from an ad hoc organization to a formal, dependable organization. A non-profit society, the Portal Heritage Society, was chartered with elected officers and a governing board. The Carter family, active in the festival and the society, transferred ownership of the still and surrounding area to the society. The chief functions of the organization have been to plan and carry out the annual festival, to hold and maintain the property, to work toward further expansion, and to promote appreciation for the cultural heritage of the region.

Efforts have been continuous to keep the educational goals of the festival at the forefront. From the outset, even the "fun" things tended to focus upon regional history and culture. Each year one Portal family sets up a grist mill on the site and gives away fresh corn meal. The Crosby family comes from Baxley to sell potatoes cooked in boiling hot rosin. (Yes, it does sound awful but it tastes great.) The best of the arts and crafts are traditional, often local. Sunday afternoons always feature local church groups in a gospel music "sing." Youngsters in the local schools have been involved through essay contests and artistic competitions with turpentining as the subject matter.

Funding is another issue of concern. The Georgia Endowment for the Humanities recognized the project as unique, innovative, and dramatic in its impact. For the second year the endowment awarded a small grant for a more limited program and brought all members of its board to the site to see the project firsthand. Since that time, several members of the Cultural Heritage Team have continued to contribute their efforts and expertise as unpaid consultants. Through sales of food and drinks at the festival, exhibitors' fees, and special projects, the Portal Heritage Society has met operational expenses and engaged in some capital improvements. However, it still refuses to reduce attendance by charging an admission fee. The amount of volunteer work on the part of a relatively small cadre of Portal people is remarkable and has always been enough to make the festival happen. All in all, the entire enterprise is self-sustaining, but it depends upon loyal volunteers from both town and college.

In terms of cultural conservation, does this thing work? What are the pay-offs? One youngster, eight to ten years old, was in a wheelchair and obviously poor. He attended the festival that first year asking questions that his father could not answer. A whole battery of Ph.D.'s gave him a personal guided tour with cross-disciplinary commentary. At the end his eyes had that special shine of excitement and discovery that teachers live to see as he said, "That's wonderful; thanks, mister."

There's a black teenager whose eyes shine too, with quiet pride in the special skills of his grandfather, who was one of the last of the "stillers" when this facility was in operation and who returns each year to help run it for the festival. Who else has a grandfather like that? And what other boy is allowed to climb up on the platform and help run the still under a grandfather's quiet direction? He is a living repository in this cultural conservation project.

The old men stop in the museum, pick up a bark hack and begin to tell "how it was back then," and curious festival-goers stop to listen and learn. The "old hands" gather in little groups to swap stories and those around them hear, question, and learn. Effortlessly, unconsciously, they preserve oral history by passing it on to representatives of later generations. They speak with pride and dignity about their part in the often harsh and difficult world of turpentining where success required skill, strength, and toughness. Those who listen view them with new respect.

Slowly but surely, the corporate memory of turpentining as a way of life is enlarged and clarified through the Catface Country Turpentine Festival.

NOTE

1. The authors wish to acknowledge the contribution of Gaynell G. Wright for the research on which the accounts of turpentine camp life in this paper are based.

Heritage Conservation and Public Education: The Ozarks Elementary Curriculum Project

William Wedenoja and Russel L. Gerlach

In a typical public school in the Ozarks students learn about the pyramids of Egypt, the Great Wall of China, and the many European wars, but they are seldom taught even the basics of their own region. This inattentiveness to the events of home is one of many factors that has led to a lack of knowledge among young Ozarkers about the history and culture of their region, which, in turn, is accelerating the decline of local traditions.

The focus of this paper is a curriculum project for the Ozarks that attempts to reverse decades of neglect of the region's culture and encourage cultural retention by instilling interest and pride among young students in their local heritage. We will begin with an overview of the region and a brief summary of other efforts to preserve its culture.[1]

THE OZARK HIGHLANDS

The Ozarks is a geographically distinct region of about sixty thousand square miles in southern Missouri, northern Arkansas, and northeastern Oklahoma (see Fig. 1). The only major highland region between the Appalachians and the Rockies, it has a rugged karst topography with hundreds of caves, extensive forestation, numerous springs, over fifty rivers and streams, and eighteen large man-made reservoirs.

Ozarks society is largely rural, agrarian, and relatively poor (25 percent below the national average income in 1985). Population density is low, and the vast majority of its approximately two million inhabitants

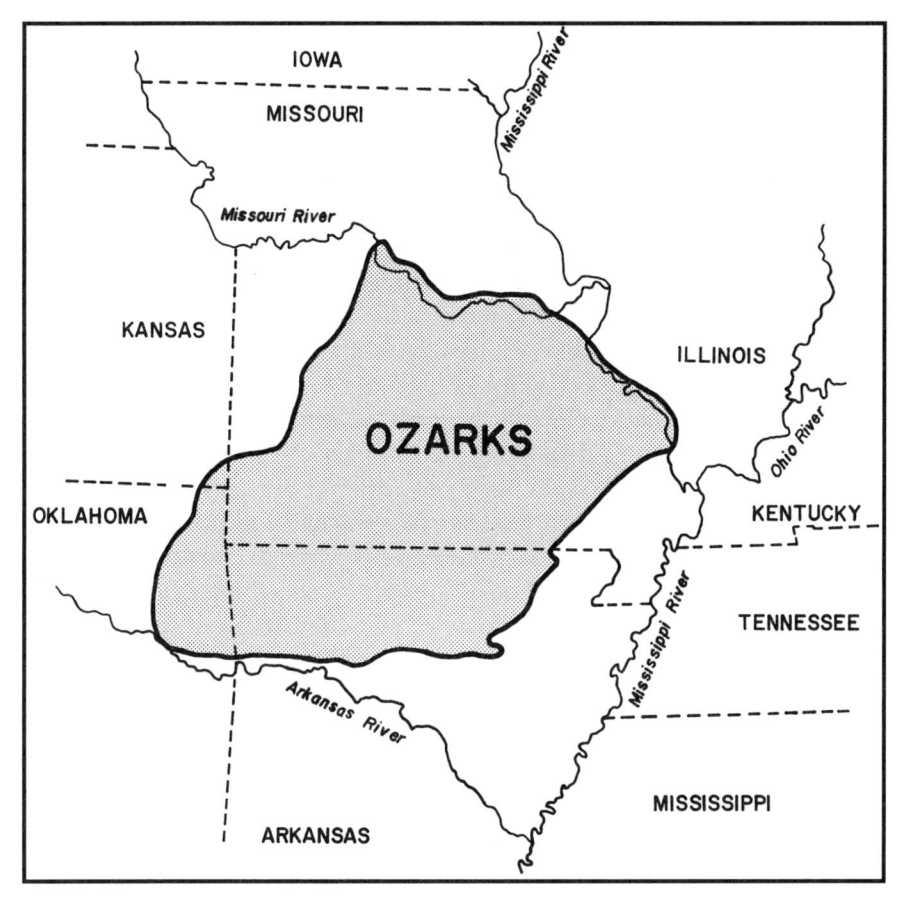

Figure 1
Map of the Ozarks Region

are white, Protestant, and native-born. Ozarkers have strong ties to the land and an uncommon sense of place. They tend to be provincial, conservative, fundamentalist, and generally resistant to change.

The ethnic origins of Ozarkers are very diverse but overwhelmingly European. Many immigrant groups established ethnic settlements in the region, beginning with the French, who settled in the eastern Ozarks in the early eighteenth century, and including Belgians, Dutch, Germans, Italians, Poles, and Swedes, to name but a few (Gerlach 1976). Traces of these heritages, particularly those of the French and Germans, can still be found in local traditions, settlement patterns, and architectural styles.

The impact of these ethnic groups on the culture of the Ozarks is, however, pale in comparison with that of American frontiersmen from the Appalachians, who were largely of Ulster or Scotch-Irish descent. The ethos of these hillman hunters and yeoman farmers centered on male individualism, personal prowess, liberty, honor, reputation, and a distrust of government and other institutions and complex organizations. They established a "thin society" with "low levels of social control" and minimal local government that was "haphazardly dispersed" and based primarily on "kin groups and ad hoc relationships among neighbors" (Flanders 1988:18–19).

The life and lore of these frontiersmen is still very evident in the Ozarks, which one of our colleagues, Robert Flanders, calls a "semi-arrested frontier." There is a strong affinity for the outdoors, and hunting and fishing are important expressions of male identity. Dogs, horses, and cattle are highly valued. Families are close-knit and reunions are popular events. River baptisms and brush-arbor revivals are still held. Crafts and skills of the frontier persist, along with old proverbs, idioms, folksongs, folktales, and folk medicine.

A Region in Transition

In recent years the living heritage of the Ozarks has become seriously endangered. An expanding economy, fueled by the development of factories and a burgeoning tourism and retirement industry, is leading to a new standard of living, new ways of life, and new expectations. Historically a region of low population density, the Ozarks is now experiencing a population explosion, due mainly to an influx of retirees, returnees, and other migrants from more cosmopolitan areas. Seasonal waves of vacationers also flood the region to hike, camp, fish, hunt, and boat in its forests, lakes, and streams, or to enjoy a rapidly expanding number of commercial attractions such as water slides, theme parks, and country music shows.

The traditional pattern of primarily self-sufficient farming in the interior Ozarks has given way to "a new rurality" in which families retain their land but also commute long distances to jobs in cities and towns (Gilmore and Flanders 1987), and farming practices are being transformed by technologically sophisticated methods, which require larger acreages and more capital. Socioeconomically and culturally, the region is becoming increasingly two-tiered, divided between those who have "crossed" into cosmopolitanism and modernity and those who have not done so (Gilmore and Flanders 1987).

Although this social and economic change is undoubtedly of material benefit to many inhabitants of the region, it is also a major threat to the cultural heritage of the Ozarks. New ways of making a living and a higher standard of living lead to the abandonment of traditional skills and, more subtly, to the decline of traditional values, attitudes, customs, and recreational activities. The ever-growing number of outsiders who come to vacation or to make the region their home continually increases the rate of assimilation of native Ozarkers to national norms and cultural patterns.

The Ozarks has often been the subject of "vague stereotypes and crude caricature" (Flanders 1987:8), particularly about hillbillies. Ozarkers are regularly confronted with negative views of their culture, not only by outsiders but also by local teachers, who frequently convey a condescending attitude. Therefore, while most Ozarkers enjoy their way of life, they are often defensive about it.

Another significant threat to the heritage of the Ozarks is its commercialization. An ever-growing number of theme parks and country music shows—including twenty-nine in one five-mile stretch west of Branson, Missouri—are exploiting caricatures of the region for profit, not only denigrating the culture but also presenting contrived, and sometimes totally false, images of it.

Conservation of the Ozarks Heritage

There is an immediate need for a systematic, large-scale cultural conservation effort in the region if its traditions are to be preserved and encouraged. Although there are strong similarities between the Ozarks and the Appalachians (the region has sometimes been referred to as "Little Appalachia"), there has been far less heritage conservation in the Ozarks. With a few exceptions (e.g. Gilmore 1984; Thomas 1981), little has been added to the pioneering cultural documentation effort of Vance Randolph, who published voluminously on Ozarks folklore (see Cochran 1985), and much of the literature on the region is amateurish, homespun, and of dubious scholarly value.

Cultural conservation should include extensive and reliable documentation and maintenance of endangered skills and activities to preserve traditions, and publications, public presentations, and educational programs to encourage their continuance (Loomis 1983:27–28). Colleges and universities can play a leading role in regional heritage conservation by establishing institutes to support and encourage efforts by their faculties and to guide and assist the efforts of communities. In addition, the mandate of state and national parks should be broadened to include heritage conservation efforts.

All of these activities have, in fact, been taking shape rapidly in the Ozarks over the past decade. Several recent books on the cultural geography of the region (Gerlach 1976, 1986; Rafferty 1980) have significantly updated pioneering studies (Sauer 1920; West 1945). A magazine and two books on traditional culture called *Bittersweet*, based on the *Foxfire* model, were published by Lebanon High School in the heart of the Missouri Ozarks during the 1970s. Two major films about the region, *Shannon County: Home* depicting traditional lifestyles and *Shannon County: The Hearts of the Children* dealing with culture change, were produced by Veriation Films of Palo Alto, California, and Robert Flanders of Southwest Missouri State with funding from the National Endowment for the Humanities. The Missouri Committee on the Humanities has provided small grants for cultural documentation and encouragement to many scholars and local organizations, including A. E. Schroeder from the University of Missouri at Columbia, for a series of slide-tape programs on "Euro-American Traditions in Missouri," and Katherine Lederer from Southwest Missouri State University, for a photo exhibit called "Many Thousand Gone: Springfield's Lost Black History."

In 1973, with the aid of a federal grant from the Economic Development Administration, the state of Arkansas opened the Ozark Folk Center at Mountain View, a living museum of folk arts and crafts that also documents traditions and provides internships to maintain them. At about the same time, Tsa-la-Gi, a re-creation of an eastern Woodlands Cherokee village, was established at Tahlequah in the Oklahoma Ozarks. Unlike the gaudy developments in Gatlinburg, Cherokee, and Branson, the Ozark Folk Center and Tsa-la-Gi represent sincere attempts to portray traditional culture in a setting almost totally devoid of commercial tourist clutter.

Southwest Missouri State University opened a Center for Ozarks Studies in 1978 and began to publish a quarterly newsletter called *OzarksWatch* in 1987. The university's Center for Archaeological Research has conducted many surveys and excavations of prehistoric and historic sites throughout the Ozarks during the past decade. A charter for these activities is provided in a proposed new mission statement for the university that recognizes "a special obligation to the public to preserve and advance knowledge of the state's unique social and cultural heritage derived from the Ozarks region."

The University of Missouri at Columbia has taken a similar course by establishing the Missouri Cultural Heritage Center "to research, preserve, interpret, and celebrate the heritage of the state and region." After five years of operation it can boast of a number of significant accomplishments: five exhibits on subjects such as tool-making and Slavic communities, a newsletter (*TRADITION*), courses in cultural heritage studies, a Missouri Performing Traditions program, a Traditional Arts Apprenticeship Program, and the Cornett Farm Historic Preservation Project.

THE OZARKS ELEMENTARY CURRICULUM PROJECT

A contemporary definition of culture, from the viewpoint of anthropology, is that it is the knowledge shared by a group of people. According to this definition, culture is intangible and alive. However, current cultural conservation legislation focuses largely on historic and prehistoric sites and artifacts, which are tangible products of past cultures. Since much of the traditional heritage of the Ozarks is still a part of the life or memories of people in the region, we developed the Ozarks Elementary Curriculum Project (OECP) to maintain and encourage these folkways.

The OECP is a multicultural education package for grades three through five that focuses on the cultural heritage of the Ozark region. The project was initiated by faculty members at Southwest Missouri State University in response to requests for curricular resources from elementary school teachers who wanted to teach about the Ozarks in their classrooms, and it was funded by a major grant from the National Endowment for the Humanities.[2] The project involved four consecutive summers of work from 1980 to 1983, and it was produced by an interdisciplinary team of eight people—two geographers, an anthropologist, an education professor, a school principal, and three elementary teachers—who shared a common concern for the preservation of Ozarks culture.

The curriculum was designed to meet several regional and national needs: to maintain the cultural heritage of the region, to counteract negative stereotypes and encourage pride in the region, to develop an understanding of the nature of culture and the process of cultural adaptation, and to combat ethnocentrism and provincialism and foster tolerance and respect for racial, ethnic, and cultural differences.

A Regional Studies Curriculum

Regional studies curricula have been produced for several parts of the country but, to our knowledge, they are all aimed at the secondary level. The OECP was designed for elementary schools because elementary teachers showed a much greater interest in teaching about the Ozarks. In addition, since values and attitudes acquired at an early age tend to persist, we felt that our goals would be better met by starting early. A cultural heritage is normally acquired in childhood, as parents pass on traditions to their children, and the inclusion of an Ozarks component in the elementary curriculum simply supplements this natural process, to ensure the continuance of living traditions.

The curriculum has three main components. The first teaching module deals with the physical features of the region. It begins with a filmstrip called "The Ozarks as a Place" and includes a wall map and desk maps of the region and a variety of related learning activities. Module 2 includes a filmstrip called "The Ozarks: People" and learning activities on the ethnic background and cultural traditions of the region. Module 3 covers the history of the region, utilizing a "Ozarks Time Line" that covers a wall of the classroom and a set of activities focusing on the Civil War in the region.

The outline for the curriculum is presented in a teacher's guide entitled *The Heritage of the Ozarks: A Multicultural Curriculum for Elementary Schools* (Gerlach and Wedenoja 1984). This book also provides substantial background material on the region, which teachers generally do not have a good knowledge of or time to research. It includes chapters summarizing the geography, history, and culture of the Ozarks and many references to additional resources such as books, periodicals, maps, records, slide-tape programs, and archives. Detailed learning activities on four aspects of life in the Ozarks—genealogy, music, education, and language—are offered as models for the development of other classroom activities. A filmstrip called "Music on the McCord Bend," dealing with the styles and repertoires of three traditional musicians, was prepared as a supplement to the learning activity on music.

A Social Science Curriculum

The OECP is not only a regional but also a social science package. The typical elementary curriculum normally includes a survey of the states and often study units on other cultures too. They can be enhanced by the addition of units on the Ozarks, since students already have some knowledge of the region and a natural interest in it. In addition, students can gain a greater awareness of both the universal and the unique features of their heritage through cross-cultural comparisons.

The curriculum was designed to foster an understanding of the nature of culture, cultural adaptation, and cultural diversity. This is accomplished primarily in the module on "Peoples and Cultures of the Ozarks," which focuses on a comparison of six populations that have contributed to the heritage of the region: American Indians, the French, Scotch-Irish from the Appalachians, Germans, blacks, and Amish-Mennonites. The cultural comparison is based on seven universal problems of human adaptation:

1. Who Am I and How Did I Get Here?
2. How Do We Take Care of Our Daily Needs?
3. How Do We Make a Living?
4. How Do We Communicate?
5. How Do We Get Along With Others?
6. How Do We Enjoy Ourselves?
7. How Do We Deal With the Unknown?

These problems cover basic elements of society and culture—identity, technology, language, social relations, the arts, and religion—in terms that children can understand, and they are couched as questions to encourage an inquiry-based approach to learning. The teacher's guide provides a model for inquiry teaching, an extensive discussion of the nature of culture and cultural adaptation, and an explanation of each of the seven problems.

A Multicultural Curriculum

The OECP was designed as a multicultural education project, to develop an understanding of the nature of cultural differences and to foster tolerance and respect for other ways of life. The seven questions encourage students to view the people of every society as members of a single species with a common set of problems, and systematic comparison of the six cultures leads them to understand that different societies have developed different solutions to these problems. The curriculum also attempts to place the Ozarks in national and international contexts, since one of the problems of regional curricula is that they can reinforce provincialism. Ideally, the OECP will simultaneously encourage pride in the region's heritage and a greater appreciation for those of differing cultural backgrounds.

CULTURAL CONSERVATION AND PUBLIC EDUCATION

One of the main approaches to cultural conservation is *cultural preservation,* which includes documentation of vanishing traditions and maintenance of endangered skills and activities. The other is *cultural encouragement,* which includes publications, public events, and educational programs to inform the public and promote an appreciation for cultural traditions (Loomis 1983:10, 27, 29). Although each is necessary for the protection of cultural resources, it seems that encouragement has lagged far behind preservation.

The OECP is basically a cultural encouragement project in that it strives to disseminate knowledge about the Ozarks to a wide audience, develop an appreciation for the heritage of the region, and generate pride in it. But it can also aid in the preservation of culture by helping to maintain the Ozarks heritage as a living body of knowledge and as a cultural identity. The curriculum exposes students to the region at an early age, when their cultural knowledge and identity are being formed, and it encourages active participation through the inquiry method of instruction. Learning activities that involve documentation or performance of traditions—such as collecting local proverbs and idioms, interviewing older members of the community, listening to old-time musicians in class, and performing "play-party" games—generate enthusiasm for learning and make it more personal and meaningful. This active exploration of traditions by students can also inspire teachers, parents, and other members of the community to develop a new awareness of their heritage and can encourage them to become involved in preservation efforts. An Arkansas teacher who is using the curriculum recently wrote to us that his eighty-six-year-old grandmother says it should have been done long ago.

NOTES

1. We would like to thank Robert Flanders, Burton L. Purrington, and Terry West for the extensive and very helpful comments they provided on an earlier draft of this article.

2. The Ozarks Elementary Curriculum Project was funded through NEH Grant #ES–*1043–80.

REFERENCES

Cochran, Robert, 1985. *Vance Randolph: An Ozark Life* (Urbana: University of Illinois Press).

Flanders, Robert B., 1987. The Center for Ozarks Studies. *Annales* (newsletter of the College of Humanities and Social Sciences, Southwest Missouri State University), Spring:8–9.

———, 1988. Introduction to *A Connecticut Yankee in the Frontier Ozarks: The Writings of Theodore Pease Russell*, James F. Keefe and Lynn Morrow, eds. (Columbia: University of Missouri Press), pp. 1–33.

Gerlach, Russel L., 1976. *Immigrants in the Ozarks: A Study in Ethnic Geography* (Columbia: University of Missouri Press).

———, 1986. *Settlement Patterns in Missouri* (Columbia: University of Missouri Press).

Gerlach, Russel L., and William Wedenoja, 1984. *The Heritage of the Ozarks: A Multicultural Curriculum for Elementary Schools* (Little Rock: August House).

Gilmore, Robert K., 1984. *Ozark Baptizings, Hangings, and Other Diversions: Theatrical Folkways of Rural Missouri, 1885–1910* (Norman: University of Oklahoma Press).

———, 1987. Toward a New Rurality. *OzarksWatch* 1(2):1–3.

Gilmore, Robert K., and Robert B. Flanders, eds., 1987. Ozarks Future Prospects. *OzarksWatch* 1(2):np.

Loomis, Ormond H., coordinator, 1983. *Cultural Conservation: The Protection of Cultural Heritage in the United States* (Washington, D.C.: Library of Congress).

Rafferty, Milton D., 1980. *The Ozarks: Land and Life* (Norman: University of Oklahoma Press).

Sauer, Carl Ortwin, 1920. *The Geography of the Ozark Highland of Missouri* (Ph.D. diss., University of Chicago). Reprint, 1971 (New York: AMS Press).

Thomas, Rosemary Hyde, 1981. *It's Good to Tell You: French Folktales from Missouri* (Columbia: University of Missouri Press).

West, James [Carl Withers, pseud.], 1945. *Plainville, U.S.A.* (New York: Columbia University Press).

Cherokee Sacred Sites in the Appalachians

Barbara L. Reimensnyder

For thousands of years the Cherokee have lived in the Appalachians. For them the earth was and is alive: water, stones, mist, fire. Everything is alive and everything is sacred. In the mountains, over several thousand years, they found places that were special for spiritual reasons. They found doorways to the spirit world; they found monsters and moon-eyed people; they found places to avoid, like the Nantahala Gorge; they found the places where sacred plants grew, plants used for healing and ceremonies; and they found places where spirits would speak to them if they fasted and prayed.

In 1838, the United States Army removed the Cherokee people from the mountains to Oklahoma. A few people remained, in hiding. Some came back from Oklahoma. At first they lived on land the size of a farm—the Oconoluftee settlement, and in isolated pockets. Today the reservation includes 56,000 acres in the Qualla Boundary and smaller tracts at Snowbird and Hanging Dog.

Many of the sacred places are not located on reservation land. Some, like the Nikwasi Mound, are surrounded by towns. Some are covered by shopping malls or airports, like the Old Katuah village which lies under Ferguson's Field—formerly a private airstrip, and the Iotla village, under the Macon County Airport. Some are on private land, like the Peachtree Mound and the Nottely Mound. Some are on National Park and U.S. Forest Service Land. Of these, some have become unusable, like the waterfall at Fires' Creek, which is surrounded by an asphalted picnic area. Some have had their nature changed: Shining Rock, where the first man and woman, Kanati and Selu, were created, is now a park. Some of the sacred places are in remote areas on government land but are threatened by timber sales, use of pesticides, and development.

Traditional people have continued to use these places wherever possible, legally or not. These activities take place quietly and often without notice. But some traditional people using government land for ceremonies have been ticketed, prevented from building fires, intruded upon, and forcibly removed, or at least forced to stop and explain their traditions to government personnel.

For the last several years, I have worked with several people and with a coalition of community groups to negotiate with the U.S. Forest Service in North Carolina. These negotiations have resulted in the establishment of guidelines for the protection of Cherokee sacred sites on the Nantahala and Pisgah National Forests (U.S. Forest Service 1987a, 1987b) and guidelines for the use of government land for traditional purposes such as smoking the pipe, using the sweat lodge, going to water, fasting, and other ceremonies. The establishment of such guidelines was mandated by the American Indian Religious Freedom Act (AIRFA) in 1978, but is being worked out on a case by case basis throughout the country.

AMERICAN INDIAN RELIGIOUS FREEDOM ACT

The American Indian Religious Freedom Act (P.L. 95–341) was passed by Congress in 1978 and signed into law by President Jimmy Carter. It states:

> That henceforth it shall be the policy of the United States to protect and preserve for American Indians their inherent right of freedom to believe, express, and exercise the traditional religions of the American Indian, Eskimo, Aleut, and native Hawaiian, including but not limited to access to sites, use and possession of sacred objects, and the freedom to worship through ceremonials and traditional rites; and be it further resolved that the various Federal executive agencies responsible for administering such laws are directed to evaluate their policies and procedures in order to determine appropriate changes which may be necessary to protect and preserve American Indian religious cultural rights and practices.

This act basically affirms what was stated in the original Bill of Rights in 1776. This act was necessary, however, because the United States government had pursued an active policy of repression towards native

American religions. In the AIRFA Report, the Federal Agencies Task Force (1979) states:

> At one time, the repression of American Indian and Native Hawaiian religions by government agents was a common practice and these religions were held up to ridicule by American society. Partly out of ignorance and partly as a result of these regrettable practices and attitudes, federal policies and practices . . . were also hostile or indifferent to their religious values. And, when the official policy of deliberate repression was ended, no comprehensive review was made of residual incidental impact of federal practices on Native American religions.

Since 1978, groups and individuals around the country have addressed issues regarding the sacredness of land, particular places, cemeteries, bones and remains, sacred objects including their possession and use by museums and individuals, and ceremonies and traditional rites (Suagee 1982). Some of these negotiations have made the newspaper while others have been carried on in strictest confidence in order to protect sites and safeguard their locations.

Legislation that we have to work with includes the Antiquities Act of 1906 as well as AIRFA. In North Carolina, General Statutes 70–5 through 70–40 provide for the protection of Indian antiquities, archaeological resources, and unmarked human skeletal remains. Laws, however, are an ideal formulation that people more or less observe; this is true for the laws regarding cultural conservation as well. While recent legislation has broken ground and prepared it, softening the attitudes of government agencies and making them receptive, this field must be worked by the people most concerned—communities, groups and individuals—not just in native American issues but generally speaking.

I have worked with a traditional Cherokee medicine person regarding some of these issues, and we have had mixed results. One local museum was willing to remove a medicine pipe from an exhibit. Another local museum would not consider such a possibility or even allow this traditional elder to view their private collection. Although the North Carolina statutes are quite clear and a young staff archaeologist, David Moore, has diligently pursued their enforcement, I still have seen Indian skulls on display in gem shops in the Cowee Valley. Traders in antiquities deal clandestinely in medicine objects. AIRFA is necessarily being worked out in different ways around the country since particular tribes have traditions regarding local places, animals, and plants that need to be addressed on the regional level because of their uniqueness.

THE CHEROKEE

One person whom I worked with, Hawk LittleJohn, clearly states that he does not intend to represent the tribal government or any group of people, but that he speaks as an individual who practices and has always practiced traditional Cherokee philosophy. He said, "Start by saying to them that to the Cherokee all things, all places are sacred. The rivers, streams, and springs are all sacred. The bottomlands, hills, and the mountains are all sacred. This is the basis of all our beliefs and how we live our lives. Tell them this first, and they will understand what it is you want to do" (LittleJohn, interview with the author, October 1, 1984). On another occasion he said,

> It is difficult to verbalize in another language, for another culture, exactly what makes a place sacred, but I'll do what I can. There are spirits that dwell in certain places that may be beneficial to a fast and helpful in other ways to the individual and to The People when one fasts and prays there. Other things that make a place sacred are what our grandfathers and their grandfathers before us have put there, or how the Great Spirit has shaped the rocks, or the ancientness of the grandfather trees, or the power of the plants. Our brothers the animals know these places and come to these places. (LittleJohn, interview with the author, June 1985)

Sacred sites can be described in Western terms as waterfalls, springs, and places of water for fasting and purification, mounds, burial places, old peace and ceremonial village sites, places of the Nunnehi—the spirit people, places related to myth and legend, and other places of special import.

THE FOLKLORIST

I want to say something about my role in the negotiation process and about what a folklorist might contribute. I have known and been friends with Hawk LittleJohn and his family for about ten years. What I have learned about Cherokee medicine has not been funded by a grant or by a job. I have been motivated by friendship, by personal interest, and at least at first by liberal guilt. Traditional Cherokee philosophy is a unified philosophy developed over thousands of years, and it expresses pretty closely the way I have always seen the world. I have participated in ceremonies and they have made a difference in my life. I have also researched medicine traditions in my own Pennsylvania German culture. There, as in Native American societies, medicine people do not put themselves forward, and in fact to step forward and speak publicly would violate the traditional role of a medicine person.

In North Carolina, traditional people have come forward because they feel that sacred sites are being threatened, and the need to protect those sites is strongly felt. Even so, many sites are still being kept secret. A folklorist can be helpful in this situation by being the one to come forward. It would be presumptuous to speak for the people, but I think we can clear a space where the people can be heard, where they can speak in a way that violates their tradition as little as possible. A folklorist can also help with the issue of defining "sacred sites" and religious practices in terms that western culture and government agencies may understand.

The sacred sites project was started in 1984 by Thomas Rain Crowe (1985), who asked me to be a consultant, along with Hawk LittleJohn. As a folklorist I have done research, helped write documents and give presentations, talked with others working along similar lines, taken photographs, developed a form for recording information about sites, and helped write several grant proposals.

In our negotiations with the U.S. Forest Service, I helped to wade through government documents, conferred with Forest Service staff archaeologists and sociologists, wrote letters, attended public and private meetings, and generally did what was necessary. Because Thomas Rain Crowe had some grant funding (from the Fund for Southern Communities) to pursue this project, he was able to devote the time needed to keep close track of Forest Service deadlines, requirements, and paperwork, and to attend all meetings.

I think that in these situations, whether Indian tribes or other communities are involved, a folklorist can be helpful. Most obviously, the folklorist can act as cross-cultural interpreter, presenting the community's values or traditional values to federal agencies in terms that fit into the bureaucratic process. (Defining "sacred sites" and native American religious practices in terms that western culture and government bureaucracies can understand is an issue of its own.) This interpretation can go the other way as well, i.e., interpreting government documents for the people. I do not mean this in a patronizing sense. Most people, whether or not they are literate, educated, and white, have a pretty clear idea on their own of what the government is trying to do, and are fully capable of understanding, in a sophisticated way, what is going on. But in this case, the Forest Service initially published a document of six hundred pages, with seventeen maps, that was intended to be obscure, by their own public admission. Also, the paperwork generated in such a process becomes staggering. At this point, I have three file boxes full of papers. Tim Buckley, who worked with the Yurok for sixteen years on the GO Road case, told me he had literally a roomful of papers. I think that a folklorist, or anthropologist, or anyone who is sincerely interested can be helpful. The problem is that the government—actually we, the taxpayers—are paying employees to implement government policy, while any individuals, communities, or ethnic groups who disagree with or want to change those policies must work on their own time.

Time is an important consideration in another sense as well. Early in the sacred sites project Tim Buckley gave me some good advice, "Plan for the long haul and don't be distracted by any excitement or supposed ultimate deadlines that may be generated." Walton Smith, the forester involved in the Little Laurel Timber Sale Appeal, offered this: "We're not going to change anything, but we can hope to stall until the next administration comes into office. Policies may change again."

Hawk LittleJohn offered some advice for anyone interested in working on these issues: "Try to talk to some of the traditional people and understand a little about medicine. Understand that these are constitutional rights that we want, that are stated in the AIRFA. Traditional people are not the same as the tribal government or their representatives."

THE LITTLE LAUREL TIMBER SALE

Two events led to the establishment of guidelines for sacred sites in the national forests. One was Forest Service presentation of a "Fifty-

Year Plan" for the Nantahala and Pisgah Forests in western North Carolina—over one million acres, and the other was the appeal of a particular timber sale, the Little Laurel Timber Sale, in Macon County.

The Fifty-Year Plan proposed different alternatives for forest management for the Nantahala and Pisgah Forests in western North Carolina. (This process was conducted in other parts of the country for other national forests at the same time.) The public reacted strongly to the Forest Service recommendations, and in public meetings and letters expressed their desire for selective cutting rather than clear-cutting, recreation rather than timber harvest of monoculture white pines, and preservation of the environment for wildlife habitat. The western North Carolina Alliance, a coalition of community groups and individuals, helped to coordinate this process and response. Respondents were as varied as environmentalists and realtors, hippies and businessmen, Trout Unlimited, the National Wild Turkey Federation, and the Jackson County Coon Hunters Association. The opportunity for comment led us to propose guidelines for protecting sacred sites and guaranteeing the traditional use of these sites on Forest Service land. Hawk LittleJohn (1984) stated in his letter to the Forest Supervisor: "My people have never had a voice in these decisions before, and have been passed over as far as decisions about natural resources are concerned. . . . I pray that there will be places my grandchildren and their grandchildren can come and pray where their grandfather and mine sat and prayed."

The Little Laurel Timber Sale concerned a tract of land in Macon County adjacent to land owned by a retired forester, Walton Smith. He also manages a 2100-acre tract of privately owned land called Alarka Laurel. The Forest Service, in a timber sale proposed prior to and independent of the Fifty-Year Plan, called for clear-cutting tracts in Smith's watershed and in the Alarka Laurel watershed, replanting them in white pines, and managing undergrowth with herbicide treatments. Smith opposed this timber sale on the grounds that not much harvestable timber existed and therefore the sale would cost the taxpayers money rather than create revenue; that selective cutting would be more appropriate on the terrain; that erosion and herbicide application would affect water sources as well as plant and wildlife.

In the process of this appeal, we found that two Cherokee sites were involved. Raven Cliffs site is on Forest Service land. This area is used in prayers and medicine formulas. The Little Laurel Timber Sale proposed cutting at the base of the cliffs. Alarka Falls is on the privately owned

Alarka Laurel. These six-hundred-foot falls are situated in a high bowl of several thousand acres of mostly undisturbed woodland.

We visited the sites several times with Smith and his work crew and with Forest Service personnel and Hawk LittleJohn, who observed that the falls were a special place for fasting, praying, and ceremonies. The Forest Service argued that their plans would not have visual impact on these areas, that herbicide spraying would not affect the watersheds, that erosion would be minimal, and that their archaeologist did not find significant evidence of occupation.

We countered that occupation was not relevant. In addition, as Hawk LittleJohn (1985) stated in a letter to the regional forester:

> What makes these places sacred to us is their personality. And their personality is made up by physical structure, by the four leggeds, the two leggeds, the winged creatures, the root, the insect and water creatures. The combination of these things give a place its personality. And then these personalities attract spirits, which have their personality. When people practice medicine and they need a certain personality to use in healing ceremonies, conjuring, or just to help The People, all the things above make this place sacred.... If you need to do ceremonies ... and you go to this place and the personality which you sought is no longer there, because some of the medicine has been removed, where do you go then? Our places are narrowing every day.

To be brief, we lost the appeal, which was taken to the local, regional, and national offices of the Forest Service. Positive outcomes, however, were that the Forest Service modified their plans to avoid spraying herbicides above the falls. Another positive outcome was that Walton Smith and the owners of Alarka Laurel gave assurances that any native people who wanted to use the Alarka Falls area for fasting and praying and other ceremonies would be welcome to do so, and that they would do their best to keep this area in an undisturbed state.

Shortly after the appeal was lost, we were able to incorporate some suggestions into the Forest Service's revised plan for western North Carolina (see Table 1), this time a fifteen-year plan extending to the year 2000. Thomas Rain Crowe, Hawk LittleJohn and I feel that this is a positive step, providing not only for the protection of sacred sites as defined by the Cherokee and protecting the confidential nature of this information, but also, just as importantly, for including the use of these sites for religious and medicine purposes.

Table 1
Cultural Resource Management Guidelines

General Directions	Standards
1. Protect cultural resources by: —Completing cultural resource inventories prior to ground disturbing or land transfer projects; —Avoiding disturbance of known cultural resources until evaluated and determined not significant; —Prescribing and implementing necessary mitigation measures if site disturbance is necessary; —Issuing antiquities permits to qualified academic institutions, other organizations, or individuals for the study and research of sites; —Protecting appropriate cultural resource properties for ceremonial and religious purposes by Native Americans; and —Maintaining appropriate confidentiality of sites.	a. Consult with Native Americans as appropriate to identify and determine the significance of sites. Contact the tribal councils of the Cherokee Nation, members of the Native American traditional community, and other interested and knowledgeable parties. b. Consult with appropriate parties (above) to agree upon measures needed to mitigate potential adverse effects prior to conducting or permitting testing or excavation at identified sites. c. Allow no activities that would be damaging to identified Native American Religious sites. d. Maintain confidentiality of cultural resources, including Native American Religious sites, as exempted from the Freedom of Information Act. Do not show locations in public documents unless agreed upon by all parties.
2. Manage to eliminate conflicts between Native American traditional and religious ceremonies and other Forest uses.	a. Allow access by Native Americans to sites to conduct or practice traditional and religious ceremonies, fasting,

Table 1
Continued

General Directions	Standards
	sweat lodge ceremonies, and other appropriate activities. b. Permit Forest use on a case-by-case basis for Native American traditional and religious activity in areas that would otherwise be closed to public use.
3. Foster public use and enjoyment of cultural resources through interpretation or development of suitable sites.	
4. Nominate significant cultural resources to the National Register of Historic Places.	
5. Protect all cultural resources which are listed on or eligible for the National Register of Historic Places or the National Register of Historic Landmarks.	
6. Ensure that all land use permits, contracts, and other Forest use authorizations contain adequate stipulations and clauses for protection of significant cultural resources.	a. Restrict minerals activity at Native American Religious Sites. Allow no surface occupancy. Require mitigation of significant archeological sites prior to any impact.
7. Consult with other federal agencies, State Historic Preservation Officer, and Native Americans for survey, evaluation, and protection needs.	

Source: U. S. Forest Service, 1987. *Final Land and Resource Management Plan 1986–2000: Nanatahala and Pisgah National Forests,* pp. III–4 and 5.

REFERENCES

Federal Agencies Task Force, 1979. American Indian Religious Freedom Act Report. Public Law 95–341.

LittleJohn, Hawk, 1984. Letter to Supervisor, Nantahala and Pisgah National Forests, June 1984.

———, 1985. Letter to Regional Forester, South Region, U.S. Forest Service, November 1985.

Rain Crowe, Thomas, 1985. Sacred Sites Project. *Katuah, Bioregional Journal of the Southern Appalachians* 8:15.

Suagee, Dean B., 1982. American Indian Religious Freedom and Cultural Resources Management: Protecting Mother Earth's Caretakers. *American Indian Law Review* 10:1–58.

United States Forest Service, 1987a. Final Environmental Impact Statement, Land and Resource Management Plan, 1986–2000: Nantahala and Pisgah National Forests. Management Bulletin R8–MB4.

———, 1987b. Final Land and Resource Management Plan, 1986–2000: Nantahala and Pisgah National Forests. Management Bulletin R8–MB4.

Cultural Conservation and Government Planning

Carl Fleischhauer

This paper is a look in the American Folklife Center's rear-view mirror, a look back at some of the folklife surveys that the Center has conducted, with an eye out for ideas about cultural resources and for connections between these ideas and cultural conservation. Although the core of our present-day approach emerged in work we did in 1977 and 1978, just after the center was founded, it is only during the last three or four years that we have found ourselves using terms like *resources* and *conservation*. These terms, of course, have come from those interested in natural resources—conservationists, environmentalists, and the like—and from historic preservationists, although we have adjusted the definitions a bit in order to suit our purposes.

We began borrowing from the environmentalist and preservationist lexicon as we learned more about their work and after we had carried out some projects in cooperation with historic preservationists. But we didn't stop there. We have also sought to adapt one of their key methods for affecting government policy, their scheme for influencing planning. We haven't worked all of the details out nor have we carried any given project to the final stage, but our schematic looks something like this:

1. Every community (and its cultural life) is affected by many forces, internal and external, including government. Some of the actions of government—construction projects, for example, or the management of forests and parks—are carried out in conjunction with planning efforts. Generally speaking, government plans take cultural resources into account.
2. Cultural resources should be understood to include not only the manifestations or expressions of culture—buildings, ballads, oc-

cupational skills, and what have you—but also the underlying culture itself, a community's knowledge and values. Field surveys can be carried out to identify and describe cultural resources.
3. If government plans incorporate the broad and flexible understanding of cultural resources indicated above, the adverse impact of the resulting actions will be minimized and in some cases the impact will be beneficial.

As we blocked out this schema, we were not only inspired by others but also influenced by our own experiences in the field. One example was a project we conducted in south-central Georgia in the summer of 1977. A team of six field-workers surveyed an eight-county area in the state's peanut and flue-cured tobacco country. The effort was carried out in cooperation with a regional arts council based at Abraham Baldwin Agricultural College in Tifton.

Like most of our folklife surveys, the Georgia project was broadly conceived; we did not limit our search to houses or music or quilts. We tried to discover an array of items that were expressive of the breadth of community life, enough so that we could fairly call the survey "ethnographic." We pursued the familiar subjects of folklife studies ranging from narrative to material culture, always with an eye out for context and for the local interpretation of culture and history.

In 1978, a team of eight workers surveyed a similar-sized area along the Virginia–North Carolina border near Galax, Virginia. This survey was carried out for the Blue Ridge Parkway, a national park (Fleischhauer and Wolfe 1981). The work began in late summer, at the beginning of the harvest season, and we documented such subjects as commercial agriculture, home gardens, food preservation, fabric-making, vernacular architecture, and the community life from church to square dance. Once again we sought contexts, local perspectives, and an overview.

These examples show how we begin our surveys with a search for "expressive culture." In the words of the legislation that established our Center, expressive culture includes "a wide range of creative and symbolic forms such as custom, belief, technical skill, language, literature, art, architecture, music, play, dance, drama, ritual, pageantry, handicraft." When instances of these forms are documented, the field-workers also record as much information as possible about the setting in which the items occur and what they mean to people. Thus the particular forms become points of entry to a fuller understanding of life and culture, or, to put it another way, the cultural resources we identify and describe include both item and context.

We may compare this approach to historic preservation surveys, which have recently moved toward an item-in-context model. A historic building must be interpreted in a particular historical setting in order to be nominated to the National Register of Historic Places. (By the way, we do not propose a register of "living national treasures." We don't think such a list would serve any useful purpose.)

Sometimes the search for items of expressive culture strikes our colleagues as "collecting," by which they mean a fifty-year-old bad habit that folklorists should break. Why not just write a good ethnography, they ask. There are several reasons, including the already-cited matter of using expressive items as a point of entry into a community. Another important reason has to do with how best to present an ethnographic report, which is essentially qualitative, to planners who prefer quantitative data. A list of concrete items (or categories of items) helps make up for the lack of numbers, especially if the phenomena listed are associated with particular locations. In addition, if reports, publications, and public presentations mention a selection of items that are meaningful to community members, like fox hounds in the Blue Ridge or boiled peanuts in south-central Georgia, then community residents as well as a larger audience will feel that local culture has been affirmed. This can engender a positive reaction and advance the cause of conservation. Finally, one may note a rule of communication: illustrate your points with specific examples. Presentations of all sorts are enhanced by the description of concrete things along with more abstract or generalized contextual information.

But what about planning itself? We experienced an epiphany during the Blue Ridge project. Our survey was progressing in a satisfactory way, but we found ourselves a little dissatisfied in our relationship with the park and with the National Park Service. This was largely due to our own ignorance about the levers and strings that one had to pull to affect the agency. We had been invited to do the project by the interpretation branch of the service and by the interpreter at the parkway, who wanted additional and more complete information about regional culture for park programs. We envisioned changes like a movement from the past-centered presentation of folklife (for example, the operation of an antique grist mill) toward a communication of the vitality of living culture.

In the end, in spite of good will on both sides, we were only able to influence small things in small ways. We learned that the National Park Service is a massive, centralized organization even as regards interpretation of local subject matter. The products we produced for them were full of information about regional folklife, but the accompanying handful of recommendations did not have much influence. We asked ourselves afterward if we should have spent more time analyzing parkway programs and writing a blueprint for interpretation.

At the same time, we came to see that the general matter of management planning might be more crucial to cultural conservation than interpretation. During the period of our fieldwork, for example, the Park Service announced plans to reduce the number of side roads that would be permitted to intersect the parkway. The plans reflected thinking about highway safety, nothing more. But the side roads and connecting segments of the parkway are used by local citizens for day-to-day transportation, and it was clear that the neighborhood's culture would be affected by the change. Residents were up in arms at the proposed cutoff and used the political process (the nation's most potent avenue for cultural conservation) to persuade the Park Service to modify its plans. The episode taught us a lesson: we needed to influence the planning process as broadly as possible. In fact, the planning process itself probably should have been examined from an ethnographic perspective.

Since 1978 we have crossed paths with planners on other occasions, and we are still learning. In 1983 and 1984, we conducted a project in the Pinelands National Reserve of southern New Jersey in an effort to influence a land-use program mandated by federal and state government, and to some degree imposed on local government. Our goal was to encourage the planners to consider cultural activities like cranberry farming, plant gathering, and hunting and trapping in the same way that they consider the impact of development on woods, wetlands, and rare plant species.

Some may wish to protect the stands of Atlantic white cedar, for example, but they should know that the timbermen who harvest them produce wood that supports everything from home gardens to the distinctive garveys that fish Barnegat Bay. In New Jersey, we have used education and communication to help make our point, producing a lengthy, illustrated final report (Hufford 1986), coproducing a book and accompanying exhibition (Moonsamy, Cohen, and Williams 1987), and supplying information and photographs used in a large number of news stories about our research. The report recommends adjustments in the structure and procedures through which land-use plans are developed. Our many public statements have succeeded in casting a brighter spotlight on Pinelands culture, but it is hard to say how much of a long-range impact we have had on the planning process.

In 1985, we conducted fieldwork with the Utah state historic preservation office and the state arts agency in Grouse Creek, a small cattle-ranching valley in the midst of great tracts of public land. Architectural historians documented the built environment while folklife specialists documented other aspects of community life. We hope our findings will guide future government activities in the area; unfortunately, we just missed the deadline for comment on a planning document for the region from the Bureau of Land Management (1985). This land-use plan will determine (among other things) how much grazing land will continue to be made available to nearby ranches—a life and death question. Many pages in the Bureau of Land Management report describe natural resources on the million acres under consideration, but only a few paragraphs discuss cultural resources, limited to historic and archaeological sites. If our report (Carter and Fleischhauer 1988) had been completed, living culture probably would have been more fully reckoned into the process.

In 1987, we joined forces with the Florida state bureau of folklife programs and the state historic preservation office to draft a how-to manual for surveying the culture of a maritime community (Taylor forthcoming). The work suggests the types of cultural features to be documented and describes folklorists' customary field methods. The manual is designed to aid anyone interested in any aspect of maritime culture, but our fervent hope is that it will advance the important goal of broadening the definition of cultural resources.

During the past ten years, the Folklife Center and various historic preservationists have sought points of cooperation and policy reinforcement, a search revealed in our collective attempts to forge a terminology for cultural conservation. The results have been helpful even though we have not yet found the perfect set of terms. One early attempt was

Carl Fleischhauer 123

the suggestion that expressions of culture could be divided into "tangible" and "intangible." The 1980 amendments to the National Historic Preservation Act categorized the preservationists' concern for buildings and sites as addressing the tangible and stated a need for attending to intangible elements like music, dance, or occupational skills. But the tangible-intangible dichotomy is concerned only with cultural expressions and not the underlying culture itself. In addition, it does not make clear the fact that historic preservationists do not address all forms of material culture; they do not document such tangibles as baskets, saddles, or quilts.

In our Utah project, we tried an alternative dichotomy: properties and "cultural features," by which we meant everything that wasn't a property. This pair referred only to cultural expressions and not to the culture itself. Culture, we argued, is revealed by analyzing information about both the properties documented by the architectural historians and the features studied by the folklorists. But the pairing of properties and features is still not satisfactory. For one thing, "features" are defined in the negative as "non-properties." And, you may ask, if one is to unify the description of culture itself, why not unify the description of its expressions?

Another problem area with implications for terminology grows out of the traditional definitions of academic disciplines. Does folklife field research limit itself to "folklife resources" in the way we imagine that archaeological fieldwork is limited to archaeological sites? Of course, recent work by historical archaeologists has broadened the boundaries of archaeology, and there is no telling where a folklorist will turn up these days, but everyone is carrying baggage from the past. And where are the historians? Just as folklorists have been typecast as ballad hunters, historic preservationists are typecast as architectural specialists. Meanwhile, historic preservation activities are hampered by a governmental apparatus that discourages looking at the recent past, let alone the present day. Disciplinary boundaries are not limited to students of culture; from time to time we encounter environmentalists who define an ecosystem as a place without human beings.

All of this has left a few of us at the Folklife Center worrying that differing approaches, training, and legislative mandates will make it hard for potential allies to work together. This worry contributed to the invention of the term *cultural conservation;* we hope that the shared ideal suggested by the term will become a common cause. We believe that the ideal will lead to collaboration in defining cultural resources, organizing surveys, and influencing planning.

Of course, improved government planning is only part of a larger movement. Cultural conservation—as many participants in this session have reminded us—will also depend on improved public education, particular actions (including marches on city hall) on behalf of particular goals, and the all-important exercise of the vote. But don't sell planning short. Government may move slowly, but it tends to move steadily and, if pointed in the right direction, its movement can benefit the various cultures that make up our nation.

REFERENCES

Carter, Thomas, and Carl Fleischhauer, 1988. *The Grouse Creek Cultural Survey: Integrating Folklife and Historic Preservation Research* (Washington, D.C.: Library of Congress).

Fleischhauer, Carl, and Charles K. Wolfe, 1981. *The Process of Field Research: Final Report on the Blue Ridge Project* (Washington, D.C.: Library of Congress).

Hufford, Mary, 1986. *One Space, Many Places: Folklife and Land Use in New Jersey's Pinelands National Reserve* (Washington, D.C.: Library of Congress).

Moonsamy, Rita Zorn, David Steven Cohen, and Lorraine E. Williams, eds., 1987. *Pinelands Folklife* (New Brunswick, N.J.: Rutgers University Press).

Taylor, David, forthcoming. *Documenting Maritime Cultural Resources* (Washington, D.C.: Library of Congress).

United States Bureau of Land Management, 1985. Draft Box Elder Resource Management Plan and Environmental Impact Statement (Salt Lake City: Salt Lake District, Bureau of Land Management).

Appalachian Tourism and Cultural Conservation

Benita J. Howell

While tourism and recreation enterprises have been important in some sections of Appalachia since the mid-nineteenth century (Raitz and Ulack 1984:236–244), tourism became explicit federal policy for the region in the mid-1960s. The Appalachian Regional Commission, established as a component of President Lyndon Johnson's "War on Poverty," encouraged tourism and recreation development projects in scenic but remote rural areas which had little hope of attracting manufacturing (Walp 1970). Appalachia also became a prime beneficiary of the Land and Water Conservation Act of 1965, which created a trust fund to enable federal, state, and local government agencies to purchase and reclaim land for resource conservation and outdoor recreation, especially to provide for the outdoor recreation needs of urbanites living along the densely populated Atlantic Seaboard (see Fitch and Shanklin 1970).

Planners hoped that land reclamation, recreation, and tourism would ameliorate both the environmental problems and the chronic unemployment typical of areas which had been exploited and then abandoned by mining or timber industries. Public ownership in national and state forests, parks, and recreation areas seemed to assure the most effective protection for natural resources and scenic attractions, given the propensity of private landowners to resist zoning and planning. Yet social scientists have increasingly questioned whether recreation and tourism can provide a solid base for regional economic development. In particular they have criticized the federal government's encouragement of tourism (e.g., Beaver 1982; Raitz and Ulack 1984:244–267).

Like extractive industry in the nineteenth century, tourism offers the greatest economic opportunities to entrepreneurs with capital to invest. The major developers are often outside corporations which import personnel for top positions and reinvest their profits elsewhere. Many of the jobs available to locals, like the industrial jobs of the past, are seasonal, pay low wages, and provide few employee benefits. Competition between developers drives up land prices, and taxes rise to subsidize expanded utilities, water supply, waste disposal, road improvements, and other county services. Natives may be forced to sell land which has been their buffer against undependable employment and leave their home communities to seek work.

These are the adverse socioeconomic impacts Appalachian people and communities have suffered in the course of private tourism development. How have local people fared in federal projects, which should be planned and managed with the public interest rather than corporate profits in mind? As Peterson describes in this volume, continuation of diverse cultural traditions has become public policy in the United States. Thus, when the federal government assumes the role of developer, the welfare of diverse cultural groups affected by development should be a concern, yet it seldom is. More often land management policies which are designed to protect natural resources and historic properties actually threaten traditional lifeways through forced relocation of communities and appropriation of their land base.

This problem was addressed in the recommendations of the Loomis report (1983:71, 76), but that report is only a preliminary step toward implementing the principle of cultural conservation in legislation and more importantly, in the regulations which actually guide agency actions. Except in unusual circumstances, environmental assessments conducted in compliance with the National Environmental Policy Act (NEPA) deal with natural resources, socioeconomic impacts, and cultural sites and properties. The lifeways and values of living communities almost invariably fall through the gaps in the environmental assessment process (see Howell 1984). Researchers have sometimes been able to justify ethnographic work as a means of documenting sites and artifacts, but this approach is unsatisfactory at best. It inevitably neglects many issues of pressing importance to contemporary communities which will be affected by impending development.

In short, current laws and regulations do not oblige government agencies to incorporate concern for the lifeways and values of traditional communities in their planning, nor is this situation likely to change soon. This does not mean that planners cannot be persuaded to take account of cultural conservation concerns, however. In fact, the environmental assessment process, which operates through litigation, increasingly seems too costly and ineffective a means of identifying and resolving conflicts. Land management agencies are now seeking compromise on controversial issues through greater public participation in planning and management. Culturally distinctive communities must be among those public participants in order to ensure that planners address the specific cultural issues which matter to them. As the papers in this volume illustrate, the range of cultural conservation issues is so broad that only basic documentation lends itself to standardization (Loomis 1983:78). Thus private citizens must participate actively in setting and working toward cultural conservation agendas for their communities.

This paper describes how citizen groups attempted to introduce cultural issues into public debate surrounding plans for two Appalachian recreation areas: Big South Fork, a Corps of Engineers–National Park Service project in Kentucky and Tennessee, and Mount Rogers, a U.S. Forest Service project in southwest Virginia.[1] Discussion focuses on issues raised by the citizen groups and their strategies for approaching the agencies, but agency predispositions to welcome or resist such overtures obviously had a substantial effect on the quality and outcome of public participation efforts.

RECLAIMING THE BIG SOUTH FORK: PRESERVATION OR DEVELOPMENT?

The Big South Fork of the Cumberland River is home to many families whose ancestors settled the region in the early decades of the nineteenth century. Subsistence farming, hunting, foraging, and livestock-raising provided a livelihood for most families until 1880, when completion of the Cincinnati Southern Railroad made industrial-scale timbering and coal mining feasible. Industrial firms bought up land along the river, built short-line railroads, and established company towns; but the industrial heyday was over even before the Great Depression began. There was sporadic talk about a hydroelectric project for the Big South Fork over the next several decades. Then in the late 1960s, environmentalists proposed that the river be left in its natural state; its white water and scenic gorge would form the centerpiece of a new national recreation area (NRA). After decades of no action, Congress authorized the Big South Fork National River and Recreation Area in 1974. It would be planned and constructed by the Army Corps of Engineers, then turned over to the National Park Service for management.

As planning began the following year, Corps of Engineers staff and contractors consulted with various federal, state, and local agencies; but they had only limited contact with ordinary local citizens. On the other hand, their site visits revealed much evidence of environmental abuse—acid runoff from strip mines, erosion caused by clear-cutting and off-road vehicles, garbage dumps, and evidence of poaching and pothunting. These observations did not predispose them toward a sympathetic view of local culture, but rather reinforced their conviction that federal ownership and regulation were essential to save the land from its former owners.

Environmentalists from the Knoxville and Oak Ridge area attempted to communicate their concerns to the Corps of Engineers in 1975, while the initial in-house planning document was still in preparation. The Tennessee Citizens for Wilderness Planning, a group with Sierra Club and Wilderness Society connections, took the lead in organizing a Big South Fork Preservation Coalition with other environmental and historic preservation groups. The coalition identified resource conservation as the primary goal of the NRA and argued for low-impact, low-density, non-motorized forms of recreation within the boundaries. They felt that private tourism facilities in the surrounding area would provide more economic stimulus for the region than would intensive federal development of the NRA itself (U.S. Army Corps of Engineers 1976:D28–36).

The coalition urged timely land acquisition to prevent continued and impending harm to resources and to minimize costs, but they nevertheless recommended redrawing the proposed boundaries to exclude five areas of plateau farmland and residences. These areas, they felt, were not essential to preserving the NRA's natural and scenic values, but their taking would likely arouse local suspicion and hostility toward the project. The coalition's response to the draft Environmental Impact Statement (U.S. Army Corps of Engineers 1976:E39–42) once again stressed these points, but to no avail. All land within the boundaries first mapped, roughly 123,000 acres, would be acquired in fee simple and placed directly under federal control. Aside from a small amount of national and state forest holdings, all of this land was privately owned.

As the Preservation Coalition had predicted, the land acquisition program engendered considerable resentment and bitterness, particularly among resident landowners. They had thought the government was supposed to help poor people, not take away their land. Other landowners who had moved to town or to better farms continued to use family land near the river for recreational purposes; restrictions on hunting and use of off-road vehicles angered them as well as the resident landowners. They saw no reason why they should be denied favorite recreational pursuits on land that had been theirs, while the recreation area catered to outsiders. Local people generally doubted that low-impact outdoor recreation would draw as many visitors as projected or create needed growth in the local economy. In the aftermath of the 1974 Arab oil embargo, there was also concern the recreation area would "lock up" resources, particularly oil and natural gas, which might be the cornerstone of industrial recovery. These sentiments were shared by a substantial number of local people; however, they did not organize to contest the plan through available legal means.

Local business people and political leaders generally supported the recreation area, motivated primarily by the promise of economic development. They wanted attractions which would draw large numbers of car-bound tourists as well as outdoor enthusiasts. The Corps of Engineers bowed to widespread local sentiment in deciding to create a coal mining museum complex at one of the old company towns, but Kentucky residents failed to persuade planners to relocate the proposed Kentucky lodge closer to main roads and existing tourist attractions in McCreary County (see Howell 1988).

Local supporters were no more organized than opponents of the recreation area until county agricultural extension agents proposed an organization uniting the rural development committees already functioning in each county. Local leaders, businessmen, and extension agents from two states and three ARC development districts formed the Big South Fork Development Association (1979) with these goals:

To plan, promote and sustain programs . . . (such as) beautification, conservation, land use, recreation, tourism, highways, job training and education, historic interpretation, public services and facilities, and business development.

To bring together individuals and groups interested in the development of the region for communication, coordination, planning, and programming.

To engage in and cooperate with investigations, studies, plans, programs, reports, and publicity related to the full development of the region.

To support timely and proper completion of the (NRA) compatible with the overall development of the region.

To support planned and systematic management and use of the (NRA) compatible with current scientific knowledge and overall development of the region.

To work with appropriate government bodies, agencies, groups, and individuals in the pursuit of these objectives.

Despite reference to beautification, conservation, historic interpretation, and planned and systematic management, the association was primarily concerned with using the NRA as a springboard for regional tourism development. The group never came to grips with planning and zoning issues as the extension agents had hoped but rather saw Gatlinburg style growth as a model to emulate (George F. Smith, Tennessee Agricultural Extension Program, personal communication, November 10, 1987). Given the association's agenda and their timing (the group organized only after the draft master plan for the NRA was virtually complete), it was easy for the Corps of Engineers to discount them as a potential consultant in planning. The association became the local sponsor for public meetings and groundbreaking ceremonies, but primarily it promoted private tourism development outside the NRA boundaries by publishing regional maps and brochures, conducting clean-up and anti-littering campaigns, and organizing waitress-training workshops and seminars on business and marketing skills. Significantly, the association was not consulted when the Park Service established policies concerning concessions, policies which will have considerable impact on the local economy and which could involve opportunities for cultural conservation programs as well (Smith 1987).

To summarize, the Corps of Engineers encountered two generally opposed pressure groups at Big South Fork: a small, poorly organized local group promoting development and a well-organized environmental coalition. In this situation of conflicting public opinion, the agency had little difficulty charting its own course with minimal public consultation. Their plan gave the environmentalists much, but not all, of what they wanted inside the NRA and left matters outside the boundaries to take care of themselves.

Neither of these groups was effective in bringing cultural conservation issues to the attention of Corps of Engineers planners. The environmentalists wanted the boundaries redrawn to save farms, but they did not attempt to bring farmers into their coalition to pursue this goal vigorously. While the Big South Fork Development Association supported certain elements of traditional culture as tourism resources (e.g., they sponsored a traditional crafts and music festival), they had little interest in conserving the culture of the "river people," who occupied the opposite end of the local social class structure from themselves and who symbolized the region's backwardness. Thus the old-timers who were conservators of traditional Appalachian culture found no allies in either group, and they lacked the skills and resources to fight their cause alone. Only a handful of archaeologists and anthropologists, who had other official business on the Big South Fork project, attempted to sensitize planners to cultural conservation issues.

The Corps of Engineers has dealt rather effectively with one special opportunity for cultural conservation at Big South Fork, however. The historic English colony of Rugby, Tennessee, founded by the British educator Thomas Hughes in 1880, is adjacent to the recreation area boundary. Rugby will be the site of the NRA's Tennessee Lodge, a reconstruction of the old Tabard Inn which drew tourists to the colony a century ago. Public buildings and some restored or reconstructed homes are owned and managed by Historic Rugby, Inc., organized as the Rugby Restoration Association in 1966. Rugby was placed on the National Register of Historic Places in 1972, and was named a State Historic District the same year. Because an active organization already had achieved this degree of protection for the colony, it was relatively easy to convince planners that existing historic preservation legislation obliged the Corps of Engineers to assess the impacts of additional tourism generated by the recreation area and to assist Historic Rugby in developing a plan to mitigate adverse impacts.

This project involved more than historic preservation, however, because Historic Rugby is embedded in a community which includes private homes, not all of which date to the original colony. Some community members have made substantial personal and financial commitments to Historic Rugby over many years, but the community also includes newcomer exurbanites in search of a permanent home or summer retreat, and members of native Tennessee families whose ancestors lived in the area before the English colonists arrived. Together these people make Rugby a living community, something like the one Thomas Hughes envisioned, rather than a museum of Victorian buildings.

The Corps of Engineers decided to underwrite a needs assessment and community plan for Rugby (Building Conservation Technology n.d.). The planning contractors worked closely with community residents, first to supplement the usual resource inventories with interviews, and later to develop ideas for the plan through a series of open public meetings and work sessions with a steering committee of twenty residents. The steering committee was representative of the various groups within the community, not only the preservationists. Committee meetings brought into the open conflicts and long-standing resentments between old-timers and newcomers, between supporters of Historic Rugby and residents who resented tourists invading their privacy. Their debates continued in public meetings, which were well-attended and sometimes stormy; but during eighteen months of talking (between July 1980 and December 1981), the factions negotiated a plan satisfactory to most. Zoning ordinances and rather stringent stylistic restrictions on new construction are acceptable because the plan clearly differentiates a Historic Precinct from outlying sections of the community, where development of additional commercial and municipal services and residential areas is encouraged. One of the more exciting components of the Rugby Master Plan is the intent to complete sections of the original colony which were surveyed and mapped but never built.

PLANNING THE MOUNT ROGERS NRA: SKI SLOPES OR RURAL AMERICANA?

The Mount Rogers National Recreation Area encompasses 154,000 acres in southwest Virginia, 111,000 of which are now in national forest ownership. This area includes the highest mountains in Virginia—

Whitetop, Pine Mountain, and Mount Rogers, which at 5729 feet is the state's highest peak. The Appalachian Trail crosses this section of the NRA. Iron, zinc, lead, and manganese were mined in the Mount Rogers area as recently as the 1950s, and timbering was the principal industry in the early twentieth century. The distinctive alpine meadows found above 5000 feet were in fact created by logging and burning and have been maintained more recently through grazing. Much of the logged-over land was incorporated into the Jefferson National Forest decades ago, and most obvious traces of early timbering have been obliterated. While farming has suffered declines in this region as in Appalachia generally, farms here are better maintained and more prosperous than in the Big South Fork region. Farming, particularly dairy and livestock, has remained a viable commercial enterprise for some communities near the NRA, but unemployment has been a serious problem, particularly since the mines closed. With few light industries located in the region, many workers had to migrate or commute long distances to work. Until recently, efforts to attract industry to small towns like Ivanhoe and Troutdale met with little success because these places lacked the commercial, medical, cultural, and transportation facilities to be found in nearby regional centers such as Bristol and Abingdon. Fortunately, rural isolation in this section of southwest Virginia was coupled with outstanding scenery, wildlife, and trout streams. This seemed to be an ideal setting in which to pursue tourism and recreation as an alternative to industrial development.

Even before the Appalachian Regional Commission was created, Congressman Pat Jennings began a campaign to promote tourism in the "Whitetop Wonderland" of southwestern Virginia. The new NRA program made possible federal assistance for this endeavor, which local leaders and businessmen endorsed enthusiastically. With the support of the Forest Service, Congress created the Mount Rogers NRA on May 31, 1966. At that time the Jefferson National Forest already controlled eighty-four thousand acres of the designated NRA and seventy thousand acres were private inholdings. Although the Forest Service planned to increase its landholdings, private inholdings would continue within NRA boundaries (Charles Blankenship, personal communication, July 13, 1987).

By February 1967, local citizens had organized a seminar to discuss the NRA project and its potential economic impacts in the hope that local businesses rather than outsiders would benefit from increased tourism. The Mount Rogers Citizens Development Corporation grew out of that meeting. Charles Blankenship, who was Forest Service planner for the new NRA, established close contact with this group as a means of keeping the public informed on the planning process, gathering public reaction and input on the plan, and encouraging local interest in land use planning to prevent haphazard development of private land near the NRA (Blankenship n.d.).

The Forest Service produced an ambitious plan for the area in response to their Congressional mandate and the aspirations of their pro-development local constituency. The plan included a sixty-three-mile scenic highway along the crest of the Iron Mountain range; a ski slope, winter sports complex, and year-round resort at Whitetop Mountain; eight recreation areas for camping and picnicking; and seven impoundments for water supply and recreation purposes. Visitation was expected to reach one million by 1976 and five million by the year 2000. An information brochure (U.S. Forest Service 1969) summed up the plan as follows:

Overall plans call for development of public recreation areas on National Forest lands with complementing developments on the intermingled private lands. The adoption of a rural motif for the private land will preserve the idea of early American rural life and use the natural advantages of the area to attract millions of persons each year.

Five National Forest recreation areas will be built within the first five years. Other plans call for a winter sports site, resort type lodges, a scenic highway, and all the things that go into making an area a top tourist attraction but without a neon light atmosphere.

Congress directed that recreation be the principal use of National Forest lands in the Mount Rogers National Recreation Area. The Forest Service will see that this direction is carried out and will work with interested groups in the overall development of both public and private lands within the National Recreation Area.

The Forest Service and local supporters enjoyed a solid consensus on the Mount Rogers plan until the Forest Service began proceedings to acquire additional acreage, some of it inholdings which local businessmen had envisioned developing privately. Meanwhile the demography and social climate of southwest Virginia had been changing. By the mid-1970s, significant numbers of well-educated, environmentally conscious exurbanites had moved into the area, attracted by its rural peace and quiet. These newcomers, some of whom were related to local families, had the will and the organizational skills to launch a campaign against what they saw as overdevelopment, particularly the scenic highway and ski resort proposals. Controversy over land acquisition through condemnation drew many long-time local residents into the opposition movement. The "Rural America" character of the area was one of its most attractive assets, not only for prospective visitors, but for local people from many walks of life. They found it ironic that the Forest Service proposed to preserve and enhance this quality by evicting farmers from their land in order to develop it for millions of tourists.

In the late 1970s, a new environmental assessment and review of the NRA plan, conducted in accordance with NEPA guidelines, gave opponents their chance to be heard. Local activists quickly established a grassroots organization, Citizens for Southwest Virginia. They secured the aid of a Washington attorney, prepared a detailed response to the plan (Blanton 1978), and orchestrated an effective letter-writing and petition campaign among local citizens. With the help of their congressman and support from environmentalist organizations, this group sought and obtained a three-month extension of the deadline for response to the Draft Plan and Environmental Impact Statement. During the response period Forest Service representatives met with civic organizations, political bodies, special interest groups, and interested citizens; they participated in open discussions on radio and TV interview and call-in shows; and they held bus tours of the area, including two weekend "workshop tours" attended by representatives of national environmental and conservation organizations (Blankenship n.d.). They explained their thinking on the plan but also listened to what citizens had to say in these meetings and in written comment on the Environmental Impact Statement.

The Final Environmental Impact Assessment and Management Plan (U.S. Forest Service 1980) identified and discussed ten areas of controversy, among them several points relating to cultural conservation: the overall scope and intensity of development, anticipated social and cultural change, economic growth, and land acquisition. Responses to the Draft Plan made it clear that by the late seventies there was substantial public sentiment to limit the scope of development in order to minimize undesirable sociocultural change. Thousands of people from every walk of life agreed that uncontrolled growth of resort and second-home developments would bring more problems than economic gains to local communities. Five million visitors per year seemed too many for the NRA and the surrounding area to absorb without adverse impacts.

Citizens for Southwest Virginia organized effectively, gained support from environmentalists all over the Southeast, and developed broad-based local support. But its lobbying effort was successful because the Forest Service made sincere efforts to implement NEPA requirements for public involvement in planning, and the organization learned how to make that process work for them. The result was a more modest level of development at Mount Rogers, a plan which would better conserve both natural and cultural resources. The scenic highway and ski area were eliminated, stream impoundments and fully equipped camping spaces were reduced in number, and scenic easements were proposed as an alternative to fee simple acquisition of inholdings. The scaled-down plan and delayed construction during the Reagan years have kept visitorship within the levels projected for 1976. Outside the NRA boundaries, very little of the anticipated tourism development has occurred during the past ten years; "Rural America" is still very much alive in carefully managed farms and beautifully maintained vernacular buildings.

CONCLUSION

Although Citizens for Southwest Virginia made effective use of the NEPA process to contest a plan which they felt would damage both natural resources and the cultural integrity of their communities, co-operation of the sort that occurred in Rugby offers citizen groups better opportunities than the NEPA process for contributing to the early stages of land use planning. Whether a group can attain the status of collaborator in planning depends on timely, effective organization as well as its policy concerns.

As the Loomis report makes clear, cultural conservation policy is broadly encompassed if not explicitly stated in existing legislation. Regulations which are already in place provide precedents and an orderly framework for addressing certain of these concerns (i.e., historic preservation), and the scope of cultural conservation planning can be expanded, as occurred in the case of Rugby. Because of the Loomis report, its legislative history, and its recommendations, there is now a sounder basis than before 1983 for forcing planners to deal with a broad range of cultural conservation issues (see Howell 1983).

What of organization and strategy? Citizens for Southwest Virginia organized quickly, mobilized a broad base of local support which cross-cut social and economic differences, enlisted the aid of national environmentalist organizations, and sought legal assistance in taking advantage of the NEPA process. But fortunately, they also encountered the Forest Service at a time when that agency was anxious to develop effective modes of citizen participation to comply with NEPA requirements. Although the Corps of Engineers developed their overall plan for Big South Fork NRA with the minimum citizen participation legally allowable and with little attention to impacts on community life, the Rugby plan was nevertheless a model of public participation and wide-ranging consideration of cultural conservation issues. Without the existence of Historic Rugby, its visibility within historic preservation circles, and the legal protection it already had secured for the colony, the Corps of Engineers would have expended no more concern and effort on this rural community than any other affected by the Big South Fork project.

Rugby's experience suggests that existing programs of cultural conservation research and public education can be a community's first line of defense when impending development threatens its cultural heritage. Research provides the data necessary to establish the existence and significance of cultural traditions; public education is essential to broadening the base of support for cultural conservation goals. Moreover, existing local organizations like Historic Rugby can be mobilized quickly and effectively to represent cultural conservation interests when they become an issue in environmental planning.

NOTE

1. The Big South Fork Folklife Survey was funded as one component of cultural resources management for the new recreation area through contract CX500090902 with the Southeast Archeological Center, National Park Service. I am grateful to Charles Blankenship, Jefferson National Forest Planner,

for supporting my interest in using Mount Rogers as a comparative case and for arranging access to unpublished documents and correspondence in 1987. I also thank Area Ranger Larry Grimes for encouraging me to return to Mount Rogers the following year and providing housing to make that possible through the NRA volunteer program. Discussion of the Big South Fork situation is based on documentary research and personal contact between 1978 and 1985 with local people, COE and NPS personnel, and contract researchers. I conducted fieldwork for a folk culture survey between 1978 and 1980 and continued to live in the area until 1985. The Mount Rogers discussion is based on analysis of published documents, Forest Service working papers, and responses to the Draft Plan and EIS. These documents are stored at the Mount Rogers NRA headquarters in Marion, Virginia.

REFERENCES

Beaver, Patricia D., 1982. Appalachian Families, Landownership, and Public Policy. In *Holding on to the Land and the Lord: Kinship, Ritual, Land Tenure, and Social Policy in the Rural South,* Robert L. Hall and Carol B. Stack, eds. (Athens: University of Georgia Press).

Big South Fork Development Association, 1979. Membership recruitment brochure. Oneida, Tenn.: Scott County News.

Blankenship, Charles A., n.d. The Mount Rogers National Recreation Area: A History of Land Use Planning and Public Involvement. Typescript.

Blanton, William, ed., 1978. Response of Citizens for Southwest Virginia to the Draft Environmental Impact Statement for Mount Rogers National Recreation Area and Mount Rogers Scenic Highway. Typescript.

Building Conservation Technology, n.d. Master Plan for the Development, Management and Protection of the Rugby Colony Historic Area. Nashville: U.S. Army Corps of Engineers.

Fitch, Edwin M., and John F. Shanklin, 1970. *The Bureau of Outdoor Recreation* (New York: Praeger).

Howell, Benita J., 1983. Implications of the Cultural Conservation Report for Social Impact Assessment. *Human Organization* 42(4):346–350.

———, 1984. Folklife Research in Environmental Planning. In *Applied Social Science for Environmental Planners*. William Millsap, ed. (Boulder, Colo.: Westview Press).

———, 1988. The Anthropologist as Advocate for Local Interests in National Park Planning. In *Proceedings of the First World Conference on Cultural Parks* (Washington, D.C.: Government Printing Office).

Loomis, Ormond, H., coordinator. 1983. *Cultural Conservation: The Protection of Cultural Heritage in the United States* (Washington, D.C.: Library of Congress).

Raitz, Karl B. and Richard Ulack, 1984. *Appalachia. A Regional Geography* (Boulder, Colo.: Westview Press).

United States Army Corps of Engineers, Nashville District, 1976. Big South Fork National River and Recreation Area Final Environmental Impact Statement.

United States Forest Service, Jefferson National Forest, 1969. Mount Rogers National Recreation Area, A Review.

———, 1980. Mount Rogers National Recreation Area Final Management Plan and Environmental Impact Statement.

Walp, Neil, 1970. The Market for Recreation in the Appalachian Highlands. *Appalachia* 4(6):27–36.

Contributors

NANCY H. BELL holds a B.A. in anthropology from the University of Tennessee at Knoxville and an M.A. in historic preservation from Middle Tennessee State University. She has been executive director of the Vicksburg (Mississippi) Foundation for Historic Preservation since 1983. In 1986 Bell was named Vicksburg's Outstanding Young Person by the Vicksburg Jaycees.

RALPH J. BISHOP received his Ph.D. in educational anthropology from Northwestern University and has taught at Roosevelt University in Chicago. He was anthropologist for the Vicksburg Cultural Heritage Project and currently works as a consultant in education and community relations in the Chicago-Evanston area.

ROGER G. BRANCH is professor of sociology and head of the Department of Sociology and Anthropology at Georgia Southern College. Since 1979 he has coordinated the public service/continuing education efforts of the Cultural Heritage Group, a multidisciplinary team of Georgia Southern faculty engaged in the study of regional and local history and lifeways.

BETTY J. DUGGAN is director of special programs for the Tennessee Humanities Council and a candidate for the Ph.D. in anthropology at the University of Tennessee at Knoxville, where her research has focused on Cherokee–white interethnic relations. In addition to spending three years as a scholar-in-residence for the Tennessee Community Heritage Project, she has also done archaeological and ethnographic fieldwork in several southeastern states.

CARL FLEISCHHAUER is a folklife specialist at the American Folklife Center in the Library of Congress, where his primary administrative concerns are the creation and use of documentary media and field research projects. His media credits include films, phonograph recordings, and a laser videodisk entitled *Ninety-Six: A Cattle Ranch in Northern Nevada*. He is coauthor with Beverly Brannan of *Documenting America, 1935–1943*.

RUSSEL L. GERLACH is professor of geography at Southwest Missouri State University. His primary research interest is the ethnic heritage of the Ozark highlands, and his publications include *Immigrants in the Ozarks* and *Settlement Patterns in Missouri*.

JERROLD HIRSCH is an Andrew W. Mellon Fellow at Harvard University. His historical research focuses primarily on the cultural and intellectual issues surrounding the development of American folklore studies. He has pursued his interest in the relationship between tradition and modernity, provincialism and cosmopolitanism, and nationalism and cultural pluralism in both academic and public sector projects.

BENITA J. HOWELL is associate professor of anthropology at the University of Tennessee at Knoxville. Her research interests and publications focus on traditional culture, economic development, and land use planning and tourism in Southern Appalachia.

SEENA B. KOHL is professor of behavioral and social sciences at Webster University in St. Louis, Missouri. In addition to serving as Scholar-in-Residence in Neshoba County, Mississippi, and examining homestead settlement in the Canadian-American west, she has researched roles of women, household and family dynamics, and processes of generational change in agricultural family enterprises in southwestern Saskatchewan.

HELEN M. LEWIS is a sociologist, anthropologist, adult educator, and former professor at Clinch Valley College of the University of Virginia. She is working with Highlander Research and Education Center in New Market, Tennessee, on a community history project in Ivanhoe, Virginia. From 1980 to 1984 she worked with Appalshop, a media center in Whitesburg, Kentucky, developing a film series on the history of Appalachia.

RICHARD PERSICO, JR. is associate professor of anthropology at Georgia Southern College. One of his main areas of teaching and research is the folk cultures of South Georgia. He has been a member of Georgia Southern's Cultural Heritage Group since 1981.

JOHN H. PETERSON is professor of anthropology at Mississippi State University. His interest in legislative affairs stems from his work as chief planner for the Choctaw Tribe and later involvement in social impact assessment with the Corps of Engineers. He was one of the first Congressional Fellows sponsored by the American Anthropological Association.

BARBARA L. REIMENSNYDER obtained her Ph.D. in folklore and folklife from the University of Pennsylvania. Her research has focused on folk medicine among both the Pennsylvania Germans in her home territory of central Pennsylvania and a variety of folks in the southern Appalachians. She currently lives in Franklin, North Carolina.

WILLIAM WEDENOJA is associate professor and coordinator of anthropology at Southwest Missouri State University. In addition to his involvement in the Ozarks Elementary Curriculum Project, he has been conducting research on personality and Afro-Christian cults in Jamaica.

MARTHA A. ZIERDEN is curator of historical archaeology at the Charleston Museum. She has conducted research in Charleston and on low-country plantation sites for the past several years. As curator, she also participates in museum exhibit and public education programs.

SOUTHERN ANTHROPOLOGICAL SOCIETY PROCEEDINGS

Nos. 1–4, 6–7, 10–11 are out of print.

No. 5, *Red, White, and Black: Symposium on Indians in the Old South*, edited by Charles M. Hudson.

No. 8, *Social and Cultural Identity: Problems of Persistence and Change*, edited by Thomas K. Fitzgerald.

No. 9, *Symbols and Society: Essays on Belief Systems in Action*, edited by Carole E. Hill.

No. 12, *Interethnic Communication*, edited by E. Lamar Ross.

No. 13, *Predicting Sociocultural Change*, edited by Susan Abbott and John van Willigen.

No. 14, *Cities in a Larger Context*, edited by Thomas W. Collins.

No. 15, *Holding on to the Land and the Lord: Kinship, Ritual, Land Tenure, and Social Policy in the Rural South*, edited by Robert L. Hall and Carol B. Stack.

No. 16, *Bilingualism: Social Issues and Policy Implications*, edited by Andrew W. Miracle.

No. 17, *Cultural Adaptation to Mountain Environments*, edited by Patricia D. Beaver and Burton L. Purrington.

No. 18, *The Burden of Being Civilized: An Anthropological Perspective on the Discontents of Civilization*, edited by Miles Richardson and Malcolm C. Webb.

No. 19, *Current Health Policy Issues and Alternatives: An Applied Social Science Perspective*, edited by Carole E. Hill.

No. 20, *Visions and Revisions: Ethnohistoric Perspectives on Southern Cultures*, edited by George Sabo III and William M. Schneider.

No. 21, *Sea and Land: Cultural and Biological Adaptations in the Southern Coastal Plain*, edited by James L. Peacock and James C. Sabella.

No. 22, *Women in the South: An Anthropological Perspective*, edited by Holly F. Mathews.

No. 23, *Cultural Heritage Conservation in the American South*, edited by Benita J. Howell.

Index to Southern Anthropological Society Proceedings, Volumes 1–10, prepared by John J. Honigmann and Irma Honigmann.